SILENT GOD

*finding Him
when you can't
hear His voice*

by

JOSEPH BENTZ

BEACON HILL PRESS
OF KANSAS CITY

Library of Congress Cataloging-in-Publication Data

Bentz, Joseph, 1961-
Silent God : finding him when you can't hear his voice / Joseph Bentz.
    p. cm.
Includes bibliographical references.'ISBN-13: 978-0-8341-2327-4 (pbk.)
ISBN-10: 0-8341-2327-4 (pbk.)
 1. Hidden God. 2. Spirituality. I. Title.

BT180.H54B46 2007
248.8'6—dc22

                                                                2007017479

10 9 8 7 6 5 4 3 2 1

CONTENTS

1

CRYING OUT TO A SILENT, SLEEPING, HARD-OF-HEARING GOD?

"It's not *you* I'm complaining to—it's *God*. Is it any wonder I'm getting fed up with his silence? Take a good look at me. Aren't you appalled by what's happened? No! Don't say anything. I can do without your comments" (Job 21:4-5, TM).

"Get up, GOD! Are you going to sleep all day? Wake up! Don't you care what happens to us? Why do you bury your face in the pillow? Why pretend things are just fine with us?" (Ps. 44:23-24, TM).

"GOD, don't shut me out; don't give me the silent treatment, O God" (83:1, TM).

Is God's voice growing fainter in our world?

If God silenced himself entirely in our lives, how many of us would notice the difference? Have we allowed the noise of our lives to drown Him out?

Our heads are filled with clamor. I recently read a newspaper article about a teenager who spends more than 10,000 minutes a month on his mobile phone. Using a wireless headset, he often leaves it on for hours at a time while he and his friend at the other end of the conversation go about their lives, studying, shopping, sleeping. At the same time, after school he is also often on his computer, juggling seven or more simultaneous Instant Messaging conversations, doing his homework, and listening to music. "I'm good at multi-tasking," he says. The article tells of another girl who spends almost ten hours a day on her phone, either talking or text-messaging. "The cell phone is a drug," she admits.[1]

Robert Benson wrote: "The way we live our lives in our cities and towns simply assaults most all of us most all of the time. The sheer unadulterated noise level is enough to make us crazy. Most of the time we do not even notice it. It has become so commonplace, so ordinary, that we are oblivious to it. Perhaps there is a contest going on that I was not told about, the prize going to the person who can tolerate the most noise."[2]

Maybe you read that and think, my life isn't all that noisy, is it? But you may be blocking out more than you realize. By "noise," I mean more than the sounds from our cell phones and computers and televisions and freeway traffic and crowds in restaurants and shopping centers and lawnmowers and leaf blowers and car alarms and our neighbors and barking dogs and hundreds of other things.

Being too busy is a kind of noise also, assailing our senses and overloading us just as much as too many phone calls and Instant Messages and e-mail can. Dr. Edward M. Hallowell, author of *CrazyBusy: Overstretched, Overbooked, and About to Snap!* asks, "How many people feel too rushed to do what matters most to them? How many people feel in a hurry all day and into the night? How many people can't take the time to stop and think?"

When our lives are so rushed, Dr. Hallowell compares us to "a tin can surrounded by a circle of a hundred powerful magnets. Pulled at once in every direction, you go nowhere but instead spin faster and faster on your axis." What are all these magnets that are tugging at us? He says people spend time

> tracking too much data, processing too much information, answering too many people, taking on too many tasks—all out of a sense that this is the way they must live in order to keep up and stay in control. . . . We have magnetized our electronic devices . . . our material possessions, our children's grades and even toys, our career goals, the laundry, the dentist appointment, the up-to-the-second news and expert advice, and even our vacations to such an extent that we have all but given away our free time, our time to do nothing but breathe in, breathe out, and feel the earth beneath our feet.[3]

Few of us *choose* a noisy life. Instead, the noise in its various forms accumulates gradually, while we may be barely aware that it's happening. Even our own minds can create so much noise that God's presence is blocked out. My friend Dick went on a two-week spiritual retreat that included group study and worship but that also allowed for extended periods of silence, up to 24 hours at a time. Meals were often eaten in silence, and no media or technology of any kind was allowed on the retreat grounds. For four days in a row he walked the same path in the hills at 6:30 A.M. On the fourth day he was amazed to hear a sound he had not heard before—thousands of birds singing in the trees above him. Not until later in the day did it occur to him that those birds "had been there the first three days as well, but I had not heard them. It was shocking to understand that 'the tapes playing in my head' had drowned out their sounds. How could I be so oblivious to what was so close, and what else was I missing because of my noise?"

If our mental clutter can block out the singing of thousands of birds, then it's no surprise that it can also shut out the still, small voice of God. As we will see in upcoming chapters, there are good ways of identifying the noise in our lives and then minimizing it so that we can invite God's presence back in. Noise, however, does not explain every period of God's silence that we may have to endure.

For some, disappointment or tragedy ushers in a period when God seems far off. His silence can descend on us during times of doubt and during times when we are running from Him. At other times we cannot point to any known cause of such a painful period. We have been following the Lord for years, but the closeness of His Spirit fades, and we feel spiritually stuck, adrift. The worship services, the music, the prayer that used to embody His presence now leave us cold. A cynicism may develop in us—toward the church, toward fellow believers, toward God himself. Where we once were full participants in the Body of Christ, we now stand aloof and set ourselves up as critics of all things Christian. We get good at pointing out all the flaws in the church and in other believers.

It's possible that a prolonged period of God's silence will be agonizing and bewildering, but it is also just as likely that, as His presence seeps out of our lives gradually, we'll be left with a dangerous indifference toward Him. Our treatment of Him may become merely intellectual, as we relate to Him at the level of a concept without the reality of a true relationship. Our faith may begin to operate only on the basis of tradition—we follow Him because we have done so for so long and it would require too much change and disruption and explaining to do anything different. We may feel comfortable in that tradition, or we may feel trapped. We slip in and out of church without touching God or anyone else. The longer this goes on, the more likely we are to begin to doubt that His voice even exists. Though we may not admit it, even to ourselves, we may begin to believe that those who do pray to Him and feel His presence in their lives are simply deluded.

God's presence and voice are subtle most of the time. Most of us won't experience Him in a pillar of fire or a blazing light or a descending dove. Even those in scripture who encountered God in dramatic ways did not relate to Him that way all the time. And almost all of them—Abraham, Moses, Joseph, Jeremiah, David, Zechariah and Elizabeth, John the Baptist, and others—endured long periods of God's silence at some point in their lives. How did the great figures of Scripture respond to God's silence?

Some accused God, yelled at Him, and cried out to Him when they felt the sting of His abandonment. The Psalms alone are filled with anguish over God's silence. Some accuse Him of being asleep: "Get out of bed—you've slept long enough! Come on the run before it's too late. God, come back!" (Ps. 80:2-3, TM). Others question whether He is hard of hearing or at least is acting as if He is: "Open your ears, God, to my prayer; don't pretend you don't hear me knocking" (55:1, TM). "Don't turn a deaf ear when I call you, GOD. If all I get from you is deafening silence, I'd be better off in the Black Hole" (28:1, TM). Still others wonder whether He simply doesn't have time for them: "Listen, God, I'm desperate. Don't be too busy to hear me" (54:2, TM).

This book grapples with issues of silence. Among the questions it confronts are these:

• What does a period of God's silence in my life *mean*? Is His silence an aberration, a sign of His displeasure, or can it serve some deeper purpose?

• If God's silence is common in the lives of Christians, both now and in Scripture, then what can we learn from the experiences of other people about how God *uses* silence in our lives? Are there things God accomplishes with silence that He does no other way?

• Is it ever possible that God is speaking to us, but He is doing so in ways that we are not recognizing? What can we do to better attune ourselves to His voice and to His many ways of reaching us?

If any of these questions strike a chord in your own life, then I invite you to read on.

2

SILENCE FROM GOD—WHY SHOULD WE EXPECT ANYTHING ELSE?

When I was a young Christian in my early teenage years, our church had a "testimony service" each Wednesday night at which people were invited to stand and tell how the Lord had worked in their lives that week. These sessions could be encouraging and helpful for me as a young believer as I heard how fellow Christians lived out their faith on a daily basis, but some of what I heard there also made me skeptical about how God speaks to His followers.

One eccentric woman who spoke regularly on Wednesday nights seemed to never have a thought or impression that did not come directly from God. How did she pick her parking spot in the church lot that night? God not only told her where to park but also arranged that her favorite spot be empty for her. He also told her, down to the most precise detail, what blouse to wear, what sandwich to eat, and what to say, do, think, and feel. It was hard for me to believe that all these details really came from God.

I've heard many other questionable claims about what God has told people in the years since then. One day one of my friends at work complained about how a woman in his small group at church had used God's supposed message to her to sabotage the group's decision-making process. The group was in the midst of deciding their future direction— what they would study, when they would meet, and other details. People offered some ideas, but this woman cut the discussion short by declaring, "God told me this is what we're supposed to do." She laid out her plan not as a mere proposal for consideration, but as a take-it-or-leave-it directive. What could the group do? Tell her God told her no such thing? Acquiesce to her divine impression?

People have tried to appropriate God's voice in far more sinister ways than that, of course. Terrorists have slaughtered thousands claiming that they were acting under God's command. Mentally ill criminals have acted out unspeakable horrors under the same delusion of God's leading.

With all these specious claims of God's voice all around us, we may begin to think it isn't safe to talk about how God speaks to us. Maybe the very idea that we think we're hearing from God means that we're either manipulative, presumptuous, or just plain crazy. Out of fear of being misunderstood, we might avoid ever mentioning His voice in our lives at all. Even more dangerously, we might begin to distance ourselves from Him. We may begin to ignore His voice or dismiss it. No need to open ourselves to ridicule by believing that He speaks to us personally. We'll be more sophisticated in our approach. No one will mistake us for one of those eccentrics. The problem is, as we shut out His voice, our faith goes cold.

God *Does* Want to Speak to Us

Despite the many ludicrous assertions about what God supposedly says to people, if we believe in Christianity, we can't get around the reality that God does want to speak to us. For many of us, His voice and His presence are what drew us to Him in the first place. I became a Christian as a child in Vacation Bible School because of the Lord's presence drawing me to Him. As an eight-year-old, I knew only the most basic essentials of theology, but I knew the Holy Spirit drawing me to Him, and I knew the truth of the forgiveness that washed over me as I went forward to pray and invite Jesus into my life. As an adult, I have worked in Vacation Bible School and have watched other eight-year-olds squirming through lessons and expending their unfocused energy on everything except spiritual concerns, just as I did at that age. Does the Holy Spirit really break through that rowdy, hyperactive exterior to speak to a child about the most important spiritual issues of life? I believe He does. I have experienced it myself, and I have seen Him work that way in the lives of other children who I would have guessed were paying no attention to Him at all.

As an eight-year-old new Christian, I didn't doubt the presence of the Holy Spirit in my life, but in a way it felt personal and unusual. Did others really experience this? It felt awkward to talk about. How could I explain it to anyone? I kept it to myself for the most part. I would sometimes talk to other believers about God's presence, and occasionally I even ventured forth to "witness" to others, but only with trepidation. His presence seemed the most real thing in my life but also the hardest to defend and explain.

God's voice in my life is still not easy to talk about. Telling about His presence and His leading and direction has been ruined by too many bad associations with corrupt and deluded people. I fear being labeled as one of those, and if I'm willing to admit it, I fear actually *being* one of those people.

Despite those risks of being misunderstood, as Christians we cling to the truth from experience and from Scripture that God wants to have a personal relationship with us. He has been speaking to human beings from the beginning. He walked and talked with Adam and Eve in the garden. He spoke directly to Abraham, Noah, and Moses. He spoke through angels and dreams and through even more unusual methods to many others, including Balaam, Gideon, David, Daniel, Isaiah, Elijah, Samuel, Mary, Paul, and Peter. He sent Jesus in the form of a man to speak directly to human beings. He sent the Holy Spirit into the lives of believers to teach them and guide them. As Jesus said, "I have said these things to you while I am still with you. But the Advocate, the Holy Spirit, whom the Father will send in my name, will teach you everything, and remind you of all that I have said to you" (John 14:25-26, NIV).

Scripture is filled with God speaking—extravagantly and in a startling variety of ways—into people's lives. He spoke to Moses from a burning bush, He spoke to Jesus, Elijah, Moses, Peter, James, and John from a "light-radiant cloud" on the Mount of Transfiguration, He spoke from the midst of a blinding light to Paul on his way to Damascus. I could give dozens more examples, but the point is this: *we can be confident that God is reaching out to us*. God's fundamental posture toward us is to love us, reach out to us, and draw us into a relationship of union with Him. This book will deal with many examples of God's silences in our lives, but those silent times are the exception rather than the rule. Fortunately, the more common experience for us as Christians is that God fills our lives with His presence as He abides with us and touches us in many forms.

One of the writers who has helped me the most in understanding the ways God speaks to us is Dallas Willard, author of *Hearing God*. Willard writes that "our union with God—His presence with us, in which our aloneness is banished and the meaning and full purpose of human existence is realized—*con-*

sists chiefly in a conversational relationship with God while we are each consistently and deeply engaged as His friend and co-laborer in the affairs of the kingdom of the heavens."[1]

Many potential obstacles stand between us and God's presence. A lifestyle in rebellion to God will put a barrier between Him and us. So will our indifference to building His kingdom. As we seek His presence in our lives, we must carefully monitor our motivations for wanting to hear from Him. Do we really want to be in communion with the Lord, or do we want to *use* Him to further our own selfish agendas or increase our self-importance? Willard writes, "God's guidance is not a gimmick that we can keep on tap for our gain. It is not there to enable us to beat our competitors. We cannot invoke it to help us win bets on football matches or horse races or to prove that something is theologically correct. While it is available to every person who walks with God, it is not at our disposal as we see fit without regard to the purposes of God's government."[2]

How Close to God Can We Get?

How close is it possible for our relationship with God to be? Think of a person who is close to you and whom you would most enjoy spending an afternoon with. While you are with that person, would you want him or her to talk to you? Of course! Conversation would almost certainly be part of your time together. But would you want that conversation to consist of the person spouting off a list of expectations and commands while you sat and absorbed it? Probably not. You would not expect to sit through a lecture. That is not how close friends usually interact.

Instead, part of the joy of your time together is that you could talk about anything you want and let the conversation follow its own course. Unless you had something in particular that you wanted to talk about to your friend, the *content* of the conversation would not be as important to you as the *connection* itself. You would not approach your time together with a list of topics to cover or a set of questions to get answered. In the best friendships and love relationships, these conversations are a blending of the selves—you want to know the person better, and you want your friend to know you. You trust the person enough to be blunt, to be honest, to be funny, irreverent, and open. That is intimacy.

Is such a relationship possible with God? It is not the way many of us approach Him. Don't even many longtime Christians approach God from a much more utilitarian perspective? We give Him our requests and wait for Him either to grant them or deny them. We "seek His will" and then try to act on it once we figure out what it is. Is that all there is to our relationship?

What is the purpose of communicating with God? As St. John of the Cross puts it, the ultimate goal is "absolute union in love with God."[3] Rick Warren states that "God wants to be your best friend."[4] Erwin Raphael McManus writes that "Barbarians [Christians] love to live and live to love. For them God is life, and their mission is to reconnect humanity to Him. Their passion is that each of us might live in intimate communication with Him who died for us. The barbarian way is a path of both spirit and truth. The soul of the barbarian is made alive by the presence of Jesus."[5]

Beyond Words, There Is Presence

What does it mean to "be made alive by the presence of Jesus"? What is "presence," and why is it so important? I think of my own children and what happens when they are hurt or sick or afraid. They immediately want Mommy and Daddy to be present with them. They desire our presence not only for practical reasons—for how we can remove the scary thing or repair the hurt—but also for comfort, love, and reassurance. Our presence is enough, even when we can't fix what's wrong. I think of what happens when there is a death in the family or some other tragedy. Our closest friends show up. They bring meals, not so much because we're hungry, not because we are too distraught to warm up some leftovers or grab something at a drive-thru, but because it gives them a chance to be with us, to give of themselves to us, to demonstrate their love. Presence is the essence of a close relationship.

That's exactly how God wants to relate to us. This close relationship is not one that detracts from God's omnipotence or authority. We should not think of Him casually as a "buddy" or, even worse, as our personal genie that we control and who responds to our whims. He is God, but He is an intimate God. We are in awe of Him, but in His presence we are loved.

Jesus spoke about *presence* when He said, "*Abide in me as I abide in you.* Just as the branch cannot bear fruit by itself unless it abides in the vine, neither can you unless you abide in me" (John 15:4, NIV, emphasis added). The words that Scripture uses to describe our relationship with God are the same ones we use to describe the closest human relationships, including marriage, friendship, and parent/child relationships. Jesus said, "I do not call you servants any longer, because the servant does not know what the master is doing; but *I have called you friends,* because I have made known to you everything that I have heard from my Father" (v. 15, NIV, emphasis added). Paul said, "For you did not receive a spirit of slavery to fall back into fear, but you have received a spirit of adoption. When we cry, 'Abba! Father!' it is that very Spirit bearing witness with our spirit that we are children of God" (Rom. 8:15-16, NIV). For many Christians, these verses become so familiar that we become blasé about their amazing content: *We are God's children. His friends. His Spirit is intimately connected with our own.*

Beyond that, we can be assured that no matter how silent or distant He seems at times, we can *know* that He is still there with us, and if we hang on, the loving sense of His presence will one day come rushing back. Paul assures us, "For I am convinced that neither death, nor life, nor angels, nor rulers, nor things present, nor things to come, nor powers, nor height, nor depth, nor anything else in all creation, will be able to separate us from the love of God in Christ Jesus our Lord" (vv. 38-39, NIV). Hebrews 13:5 records God's promise, "I will never leave you or forsake you."

It is possible, as Willard puts it, for our relationship with God to move from *communication* with Him toward *communion* and *union* with Him. He explains that we can *communicate* even with our enemies, but when we move toward *communion*, "there is a distinctness, but also a profound sharing of the thoughts, feelings and objectives that make up our lives."[6] Beyond even that close relationship is *union*, when the two partners, as in a marriage relationship, are linked together even more inextricably: "It is this union beyond communion that Paul speaks of when he says the redeemed have the mind of Christ (1 Cor. 2:16) as well as when he exhorts us to have the mind of Christ (Phil. 2:5). Jesus prays the faithful might have this same union: 'that they may be one, as we are one, I in them and you in me, that they may become completely one, so that the world may know that you have sent me and have loved them even as you have loved me' (John 17:22-23)."

Where Do We Find God's Presence?

Part of me desires this union with God more than anything—why wouldn't I? I know the power, the love, the joy that comes from basking in His presence. So why do I find myself sometimes avoiding what takes me there?

One reason I may sometimes think of God as silent in my life is that I limit my perception of His Spirit to only one or two activities or contexts. I may miss His voice in other places because I'm simply not attuned to it.

Mother Teresa told an interviewer that the poor people she served were God's greatest gift to her because they allowed her the opportunity "to be 24 hours a day with Jesus." She explained, "The dying, the crippled, the mentally ill, the unloved—they are Jesus in disguise."[7] Do I experience Jesus in those I serve? Do I see Him in the faces of my friends, my children, my wife, my neighbors, my coworkers, my fellow church members? God is present in those around me.

I have a Bible on my desk. Does it stay there, or do I open up the book and invite God to speak to me from those pages? Do I approach the words not simply looking to bolster my own ideas or to prove something, but rather to know and understand God better? Do I allow the words to penetrate me and change me?

I have a church that I go to regularly. Do I go there ready to find God, to hear Him and feel His presence and worship Him with fellow believers? Do I open my spirit to the messages from the pastors and the small groups and the musicians?

Do I spend deep time in prayer, not simply asking God for things but also quieting my inner self enough to really listen to Him? Do I pray without ceasing, turning to Him throughout the day, seeking His guidance and acknowledging His Spirit?

Do I search for Him in the beauty of the moment—the play time with my children, the phone call from a distant friend, the date with my wife, the pleasure of an early morning run? God's Spirit suffuses my life. Am I listening?

With all the ways that the presence of God can be part of our lives, it might seem that we would never lose our sense of His presence, and yet we do. We will consider many reasons for this, some of which are out of our control. However, one reason our sense of God's Spirit fades is that His voice gets lost in the cloud of static with which we have surrounded ourselves, a dilemma we'll look at in the next chapter.

Questions for Reflection

1. Most of us have heard people make bizarre and unbelievable claims about what God has supposedly told them. Have those kinds of absurd claims ever made you reluctant to talk about how God speaks into your own life as a Christian? How can you discern the difference between someone's claim of hearing from God that is false, manipulative, evil, or self-seeking, compared to a claim of hearing God's voice that is a natural part of knowing the Lord as a follower of Christ?

2. This chapter talks of the Christian life as being one of "union with God." Describe what that union is like in the life of a Christian who is living it. What activities, attitudes, habits, and character traits will be evident in such a person?

3. The final section of this chapter makes the point that we sometimes overlook God's presence because we limit our awareness of Him to only one or two contexts and activities and are not attuned to the many ways and places in which He is present. Consider in what contexts you are most likely to sense God's presence. In what context mentioned in that section are you most likely to overlook Him? What can you do to make yourself more aware of Him?

IS GOD TOO QUIET, OR IS THE WORLD TOO NOISY?

I love watching movies, but the theater experience can be frustrating, with people breaking the intensity of the experience with their chatter and with the occasional cell phone sounding off. Not long ago, I seethed in my theater seat as a cell phone chirped in the middle of one of the best scenes of the movie, followed by a teenage voice repeatedly hissing into the phone, *"I can't talk! I'm in a movie. What do you want? I can't talk! I'm in a movie!"*

On my next movie outing, however, people were better behaved. Not a single phone broke the mood, and the audience kept their yapping to a minimum. The surprising part, though, was what happened once the movie ended. The theater was crowded, and the closing credits were very dark. After we snaked our way through the corridor and emerged into the bright lobby, I looked up to see a sea of people lunging for their phones, punching the buttons as if the little devices contained lifesaving oxygen that their owners would soon expire without. To have been cut off—deprived!—of this connection to the outside world for two solid hours was clearly almost more than many of these movie-watchers could take. They clung to their phones as if the very secrets of the universe were being pumped into their heads.

Whenever I see a movie, I like some time afterward to mull it over and maybe talk about it with someone over a cup of coffee. Part of the pleasure of the experience for me is getting *away* from phones and e-mail and other distractions, but in that crowd I was in the minority. For most of these phone-talkers, that experience was over the second the credits started to roll, and they had already moved on to the next thing. As they walked off with their phones pressed to their ears, they even seemed to be finished with the people they had come with.

A few days later, my wife and I had a rare lunchtime date during the workday at our favorite Thai restaurant. The atmosphere was a relaxing change from the hectic pace of the office. The lights were dim and the room was quiet except for soft music and the murmur of the other diners' voices. We talked, sipped our sweet Thai iced tea, enjoyed the smell of delicious food all around us, and waited for our meal to arrive.

Then the Realtors barged in. The two women chose a booth near us and bellowed out the details of their latest transactions to each other, oblivious to how much louder their voices were than every other sound in the dining room. But that turned out to be the quiet part of their meal. Soon their phones started going off, and they spoke even louder into those, issuing commands to secretaries and confirming appointments. Then, as if they had not disrupted all of our meals enough, they took one call on a speaker phone in the middle of the table between them.

Now there were *three* voices vying to out-rant one another as each woman tried to gain dominance in the conversation by raising the volume of her voice over the other two. "We need to move on this *now*!" one agent bellowed to the entire restaurant. Just in case there might have been a waitress or cook in the kitchen who failed to hear this declaration, she repeated it at least three times during the conversation. The tinny, disembodied voice in the center of the table had her favorite phrase too: "We could work the deal either way!"

As the disagreements among the women increased, the stress level in the entire room rose, and it was nearly impossible for us to focus on our own quiet conversations. The dealing and wheedling and cajoling was still going on when we left, and the women showed no sign that they were aware that most of the other diners in the restaurant had come there to get away from the noise of an office, not to enter someone else's work space.

These scenes, though annoying, should not surprise me. Almost no place is exempt anymore from the intrusion of other people's phone conversations. It is rare that a phone does not go off in our church service, even though a request to turn them off is part of every announcement time. At the university where I teach, I have recently had to add a statement to each syllabus banning all electronic devices in the classroom. Otherwise, the students' concentration is constantly interrupted by phones, e-mail, Internet pages, and music from the earphones they try to subtly hide in their ears (even though they insist, when challenged, that none of these distractions prevent them from being involved in class discussions).

It might be easy to dismiss all this as nothing more than examples of bad manners, but does it indicate a larger problem? What are the unintended consequences when we spend almost every waking (and sometimes sleeping) moment with our brains being bombarded by outside stimulation? What happens to quiet contemplation? What happens to silent walks or jogs to think things through? What happens to intimate moments of prayer? Can we listen for God if our minds are already bursting with so much other noise? Psalm 46:10

says, "Be still, and know that I am God!" Is that even possible for us? Without being fully aware of it, do we push our lives in the opposite direction, filling every moment with some-thing—anything—that will vanquish the silence?

Certainly much of the noise is pleasant, and some of it is necessary. We may like music when we walk. We like keeping in touch with people by phone and e-mail. We like going to our kids' loud baseball games. We have duties to our families and our employers.

But the noisy lifestyle is addictive in many ways, and it can turn corrosive, harming us intellectually, creatively, and spiri-tually. How? Social commentator Carl Honore, author of *In Praise of Slowness: Challenging the Cult of Speed,* discusses the relaxed state of mind, which he refers to as Slow Think-ing, that produces the best creativity and thought. He points out that research confirms that people are most creative when they are calm, free from the "noise" of stress, and have plenty of time to think. His personal experience matches the re-search findings: "My eureka moments seldom come in a fast-paced office or a high-stress meeting. More often they occur when I am in a relaxed state—soaking in the bath, cooking a meal or even jogging in the park."[1]

Some of the most creative people in history also found the need to reduce the "noise" and speed of life in order to allow for their best insights. Honore writes, "Albert Einstein was fa-mous for spending ages staring into space in his office at Princeton University. In the stories of Arthur Conan Doyle, Sherlock Holmes weighs up the evidence from crime scenes by entering a quasi-meditative state, 'with a dreamy vacant ex-pression in his eyes.'"[2]

But Albert Einstein and Arthur Conan Doyle lived before

the noisy age of 24-hour news channels, mobile phones, and e-mail. Wouldn't the smartest and most successful people of today more likely be multitaskers surrounded by the most cutting-edge technological gadgets and time-saving electronic devices money can buy? Edward Hallowell answers "Warren Buffett sits at his computerless desk in Nebraska and thinks. Bill Gates takes two weeks off every year to go to a cabin in the woods to . . . think. An unknown but talented poet sits somewhere right now in silence, grappling with his imagination to find the right word. Two lovers sit silently side by side in chairs by a lake right now, connecting intimately without speaking. . . . In fact, busy is not always best."[3]

What mind-set does it take to achieve the kind of intimacy with God discussed in the previous chapter? If prayer is to be a time of connecting and conversing with God rather than our quick presentation of our list of requests, then what state of mind do we need? If we are to have the time and motivation to open the Bible in the first place, and then take time to let the words sink in deeply as God speaks to us through them, how calm and undistracted do our hearts and minds need to be?

In order to reach a state in which we can consistently hear God's voice and achieve intimacy and union with Him, we may need to reduce the competing noises in our lives. One danger is that *without our realizing it,* the noise that engulfs us may have already weakened our connection to God so much that He is barely a presence in our lives. This distance between us and Him may have existed for so long that we consider it normal. We think, isn't God such a faint presence in *all* Christians' lives? Isn't that a reality we simply have to accept?

Before I more closely examined my own life, I was under the impression that it was much less noisy than it really was.

Rather than reducing the noise, I had instead found ways of managing it or ignoring it. We all have to do that to some extent, and certainly it's possible for God to speak to us in the midst of chaos, just as it's possible to conduct a telephone conversation while the baby in my arms is screaming or to eventually fall asleep even though the music from the neighbor's party is shaking the walls of my home. But wouldn't that phone conversation go better if someone took care of the baby while I went into the next room, and wouldn't the sleep come easier and better if the walls stopped vibrating and quiet filled the night air?

Before we consider specific ways that we can cut down the noise in our lives in order to hear God better, it may be helpful to first look at the many types of noise that threaten to overwhelm us—from the physical sounds we unconsciously block out to the interior clamor that keeps our minds in turmoil.

Physical Noise: Blocking Out Sound That Leaves Us Sleepless, Distracted, and Irritated

The meeting got off to a bad start. A guest speaker that I had invited to our university stood up to speak to a group of about 50 of our students who had gathered to hear her in one of the worst rooms in our school—a "dining room" separated from the main student cafeteria by a thin accordion-style partition that blocked out little noise but that could be snapped shut to give the illusion of privacy.

I had scheduled the event for 7:30 P.M., hoping most of the cafeteria dinner crowd would be gone by then. They were, but the clean-up crew was just getting started. No problem, I thought. How noisy could they possibly be?

Their blood-chilling shrieks were my answer to that question.

I had no idea that cleaning tables could be so much fun! It's not a job, it's a sport, involving screaming and laughing and throwing things at one another. From my side of the partition, I couldn't quite figure out what objects they were flinging at each other, but it sounded like tables or chairs crashing to the floor. Following each crash, the winning team let out a whoop of joy, and then a new round began.

Our speaker made a little joke about the screaming and continued her presentation. I considered opening the partition to ask them to quiet down, but I knew that would be even more distracting than the noise itself. The only other way to get to them was by a winding path through the building, and I hoped the noise would stop without my having to disrupt the meeting by walking out.

The table-crashing game stopped within a few minutes, and I relaxed. But then came the opera singer. Just beyond the partition, one of the workers, apparently a music major, decided to practice an aria as she wiped off the tables and straightened the salt and pepper shakers. Her voice was beautiful, but it didn't blend well with the speech our audience was straining to hear. To make matters worse, someone started to play the piano that resided in the corner of the cafeteria. I could sit still no longer. I got up and wound my way toward the cafeteria to ask for an end to the noise.

A few minutes later I returned, having quieted down an embarrassed cleaning crew who hadn't realized we were there. Now I could settle down and enjoy what remained of the speech. Except that one floor above us, in a room that housed the university's chapel services, a band began to play.

Not a quiet, subdued band, but one with drums and electric guitars and full-throated singers. The ceiling quivered.

Before I could figure out what to do about that sound, someone pulled up in a car on the road just outside our building and honked furiously, apparently trying to get someone's attention.

By that time my own frustration level was so high that I was ready to jump up and make some noise of my own by apologizing to the speaker, canceling the speech, and going home.

But then I noticed something. *Almost none of the students in the audience seemed disturbed by the noises that surrounded them.* They looked straight ahead at the speaker, trying to focus on what she was saying. Were they really able to filter out all that chaos? If so, how had they learned to do it?

The answer was right in front of me. These were college students, most of whom lived crammed together in residence halls with two or three people in each room. Almost their entire existence consisted of being bombarded by other people's music, conversations, telephone calls, laughter, TV shows, hair dryers, computer printers, video games, and dozens of other sounds. Many of them went entire days without enjoying a minute of silence. Even their nights were filled with noise as roommates and neighbors kept the music, talk, and other sounds going almost round the clock.

These students might show up bleary-eyed to their morning classes, but they still would say the noise didn't bother them. *What* noise, they might ask. They get so good at filtering it out that they are no more aware of it than of the air they breathe. They suppress the noise automatically, a mechanism to gain some sense of focus and concentration in a frenzied world.

But I wondered, what else are they—or any of the rest of

us—filtering out unintentionally? In the long run, what impact does all this racket have on us spiritually? The students *manage*, but when do they have time for reflection, for listening, for those unfilled moments of ruminating on plans and visions, pondering where God may be taking them and where they have been? As they scurry from one noise to another, keeping chaos at bay, will God's voice be one of those sounds that gets squeezed out?

Even for those of us with good noise filters, sometimes the noise level grows beyond our ability to block it out, leading to anything from irritation to despair. A few years ago a freeway that had once ended near my home was extended to go many miles beyond it, shattering the relative quiet of all the residents who lived in its path. Even though the extension had been planned for years, many who lived near it were stunned by how much the roar of the thousands of cars and trucks hurtling across the pavement day and night disrupted the tranquility of their daily lives.

Outraged citizens of towns along the freeway route raised an uproar in every city and state government office they could find. I read newspaper stories about people trying to buy soundproof windows and take other measures that might block at least part of the sound. I read about one woman who burst into tears because of lost sleep and the frustration of never being able to turn off or even turn down the noise. Houses for miles around went up for sale, their value now reduced. Politicians and engineers tried to calm people's anger, though there wasn't much they could do.

One day my wife and I received a letter in the mail inviting us to join a class action lawsuit to seek damages because of the noise of the freeway. I had sympathized with those whose stories I had read in the paper, but my first thought was, do we even *hear* the freeway at our house? We were enough blocks away from it that we couldn't see the freeway or, I thought, couldn't really hear it.

But then I went to the window and listened.

I heard the distant hum. Occasionally the rumble of a semi-truck broke in a little louder over the normal buzz of traffic. That night, in bed with our windows open, I heard the noise even louder. With the normal daytime sounds of the neighborhood reduced, I could even distinguish fluctuations in the flow of traffic and pick out the sounds of individual motorcycle and truck engines. Why had I never noticed this before? Why had it never bothered me? As a child, I had grown up within sight of a freeway, and yet now I don't really remember noticing that sound either.

The reason the freeway noise didn't bother me was that it had never reached the level where I couldn't block it out. We didn't join the lawsuit. If we started suing people for making our world too noisy, where would that end? The list would be too long. People who visit our home often comment on what a "quiet neighborhood" we live in, and compared to some other places where people live, I suppose that's true. Yet here are just some of the sounds that I can hear in this "quiet" place if I sit for a while at my window: lawnmowers, leaf blowers, airplanes, cars and trucks, car alarms, hammers pounding on wood, electric saws and drills, dogs barking, children laughing and yelling, blaring radios. Inside my house, I can hear a washer and dryer, dishwasher, flushing toilet, television, telephone, the voices of my wife and children, my son's video game, my daughter's screeching toy microphone, loud music from the stereo, the doorbell, the furnace or air conditioner.

If I were to extend this list beyond the "quiet" home to workplaces and other public spaces, the list could go on for many pages. How many sounds assault you in a factory, a restaurant, a shopping mall, a school, a gym, a playground?

By themselves, none of these noises is a problem. I certainly wouldn't want to silence them all. I thank God that I am capable of hearing them. But it makes me wonder, if I can hear all this and yet still consider it "quiet," how much of my mental energy is being diverted toward blocking out this sound? And even though I am *able* to block out much of it, could it still be harming my concentration anyway?

Have you ever been trying to think or sleep, but *one noise* keeps annoying you? One afternoon I sat in my office and listened to a car alarm wailing in a nearby parking lot. I had papers to grade, so at first I tried to ignore it. Surely somebody would soon turn it off, I thought. It shrieked on and on. I set my papers aside and took care of a few other little chores that took less focused attention. The high-pitched screech continued. I eventually got back to the paper-grading, since I couldn't afford to lose an entire afternoon to this nuisance. I was able to get *some* work done, but I was never able to sink into the *true* concentration I needed, that focus of mind that is relaxed and unforced, in which I didn't have to guard my thoughts against the onslaught of noise.

I've had similar experiences with sleep. I once stayed in a hotel in which I heard the grinding roar of some kind of air conditioning unit just outside my closed window. I tried to ignore the relentless drone, but it was too loud to simply block it out. I covered my ears with a pillow, but the sound came through anyway. I eventually got up and watched some TV for a while, thinking that if I got tired enough, I would sleep in spite of the noise. I considered asking for a different room, but I didn't want to go to all that trouble in the middle of the night. The machine rumbled on. I did eventually lie back down and manage to sleep, but the noise got tangled up in my dreams, and the sound of the monster kept jolting me miserably awake.

Sometimes noise can be so disturbing that people go to bizarre lengths to stop it. The *Los Angeles Times* reported on packs of sea lions that have invaded Newport Beach and other communities along the West Coast. The barking of the sea lions is so loud that it has turned residents "into sleepless zombies." One resident said, "A barking dog doesn't hold a candle to this. It's like 40 barking dogs—in surround sound."[4] Residents have tried all kinds of methods to get rid of the sea lions, including fake whales submerged in the water like an aquatic scarecrow, underground speakers to blast high-pitched sounds at them, rubber bullets, firecrackers, and a motion-sensor device that pelts the intruders with water. None of it has worked.

Noise is not the only problem with the sea lions—they have also attacked people and damaged boats—but residents find that they often get little sympathy from outsiders about how disruptive the sound of the animals' barking is. One sleep-deprived resident said, "People probably think, 'Oh, you live on the water, you have a beautiful life, quit your complaining, this is part of living on the water.' But this is far beyond normal-sounding sea life."[5]

Such a dismissive attitude is common, isn't it? We're not really supposed to mind the concentration-breaking, sleep-stealing noise. Isn't it simply a part of life that we can't do anything about? Some people live with it so long they no longer even *want* to get rid of it. People who are used to having the television on all the time for background noise get very uncomfortable when it is turned off. People who are used to a blaring TV volume are frustrated when it's turned down to a more conversational level, even though they can easily hear it.

In one New York City neighborhood, an elevated train has rumbled through town every day for almost a hundred years. The clatter is so loud that when the train passes overhead, people have to stop conversations—and thought—for about 20 seconds until it passes. Visitors to the neighborhood sometimes cover their ears. Last year a workers' strike brought the train temporarily to a halt, and residents enjoyed relative quiet for the first time in their lives. Some welcomed the respite. One neighbor said, "The noise is so annoying, I hope the strike lasts forever. It's a whole other world without those things going by."

Oddly enough, however, some people missed the bone-jarring sound. One man said, "It's strange, but the silence is more noticeable than the noise. When you spend your life hearing the screech of steel wheels over your head every two minutes, you almost forget what quiet is." A mail carrier in the area told the *New York Times*, "You learn to block it out normally, but it's always there," and complained that his day now "feels like a funeral procession."[6]

People cope with noise in all sorts of ways—filtering it out, fighting it, resigning themselves to it—but what would it be like to spend time in a place that is *truly* quiet? Do such places exist? One man specializes in finding them. Gordon Hempton, an acoustic ecologist, defines a quiet place as a spot "where you can go and listen and not be distracted by human-caused noise."[7] To qualify for his list of quiet places, the sounds of nature must be undisturbed in that area for at least

15 consecutive minutes during daylight hours. How many quiet places would you guess still remain in the United States?

Surprisingly, by that definition *only seven or eight* quiet places remain in the United States. In Europe, there are none. Some other remote areas come close but are disqualified because of the sound of airplanes. But the number of quiet places has rapidly declined over the last two decades. In Washington State alone, Hempton found 21 quiet places in 1984, but 10 years later, only 3 were left.

Hempton has recorded the sounds of undisturbed nature on 60 compact discs that people can buy. Often when people listen to them, they fall asleep, but he doesn't mind. As he told *L.A. Times* reporter John Balzar, "Hearing is our surveillance system. Hearing doesn't have a blind side. We don't need any instruction; our hearing tells us when we are in a secure, peaceful place. So when someone listens to my work and nods off, I say, 'Yes, I know what you mean. I've been there.'"[8]

If hearing is our surveillance system, then what effect does all the daily noise of traffic and televisions and sirens and crowds have on us? Hempton says that the noise overwhelms our inborn audio radar. As Balzar explains, "We end up filtering out our environment, but we cannot entirely shut down our defense system. It is the worst of both worlds, leaving us to stew in perpetual anxiety and stress."

As spiritually distracting and destructive as physical noise can be, there is another kind of noise that can harm us even more, which we'll discuss in the next chapter.

Questions for Reflection

1. This chapter mentions many noises that people find particularly irritating, such as people talking in theaters, cell phones going

off in church, blaring car alarms, traffic noises that keep people awake at night. Which noises do you find particularly bothersome, and why? What happens to your state of mind if you are bombarded by these sounds for too long?

2. Pick a place you think of as quiet. Sit there silently for 15 minutes and make note of all the sounds you hear. How quiet is it really? Are you surprised by how many sounds you hear?

3. Do you sense that the world is noisier than it used to be? If so, what noises are either new or are more prominent in your life than in years past?

4. Make a list of all the noises you have to block out during the day in order to be able to concentrate, relax, conduct business, or pray. Do you agree with the chapter that the noisier your life gets, the more likely you are to block out or ignore God's voice even when you don't realize you're doing so? In what ways can too much noise affect your spiritual life?

DROWNING IN AN ELECTRONIC FLOOD

I sit in my office in the middle of the afternoon. This is the two-hour block I've been looking forward to, when my schedule is free to allow me to give some careful, focused attention to a writing project whose deadline is fast approaching. The computer is on, the document is open, my materials are gathered around me, my fresh cup of coffee is poured. I am ready to dive in.

In order to prevent any distractions while I work, I decide maybe I should quickly check my e-mail to make sure there's nothing urgent that needs my attention. I've already checked it a few times, but I've been waiting on some answers to a couple things, and you just never know when they might pop up. I feel the rush of anticipation as I type in my password.

There are e-mails all right, but not the ones I was looking for. Most of these can wait. I need to get back to work. Still, a couple of these look too intriguing to pass up, so I'll click on them and see. Looks like I could answer these quickly and get them off my mind before I get back to work. But first, while I'm on the Internet, I might as well check the news. I haven't seen what's happening all day. I try one site, but it doesn't have much. No problem. I have three or four other sites that I can quickly cycle through to at least glance at the headlines.

But wait. Here's an article that might be useful in my research one of these days. Maybe I'd better take a couple minutes to read through it. I click on it, but as I do, I happen to glance over to see that the message light on my phone is on. Why didn't I notice that before? Better check it. Could be an emergency. I pick up the phone and listen to the message. It's far from an emergency, but I write down the number to return the call later. Time is slipping away. I need to get started on my writing. This is the only time I'll be able to do it today.

But first, that article I was about to read. I skim through it. It's hard to concentrate on it. I feel guilty for wasting time to read it, but I don't want to forget about it either. I'll save it and read it later. There. Now back to my writing. Oh, I forgot. I was going to answer those e-mails real fast. Oh no! Now the phone's ringing. I should let it go to voicemail. If I start talking on the phone, I'll never get any work done. On the other hand, it might be an emergency. I guess I'll answer it.

Well, there goes another 10 minutes. I shouldn't have picked it up. Finally now, time to dig in to the work. Oh no. A knock on the door. Shouldn't take long. I see she's mouthing "just a minute" through the window.

Well, the first hour of my writing time is gone, but I still have one more. Better make the most of it. Did I send those e-mails? Better check. Looks like I got a couple new ones. I've spent so much time on this already, I might as well read them.

Sound familiar?

Many of us spend much of our days this way, with our thoughts chopped into little pieces as we jump from e-mail to phone call to quick conversation back to e-mail and then off to some Web sites. All the while our frustration builds because those things in our lives that require blocks of time or unhurried focus—such as meaningful work, a satisfying conversation with a friend, deep prayer, attentive study of God's Word—get postponed, rushed through, or set aside altogether.

We've already examined how disruptive *physical* noise can be to our ability to concentrate, but the greater danger for most of us is that we will spend our days also frazzled by the *psychological* noise of too many TV voices, too many interrupted conversations, too many electronic devices vying for our attention, too many fragmented thoughts. Many of us do not even *try* to quiet this noise. In fact, we can't get enough of it. Some get so caught up in filling our minds with this alluring flood of words and images that it leads to outright addiction.

The manager of a hotel in Chicago recently started his own program to help guests manage their addictions to their BlackBerrys, the handheld communication devices that allow people to check e-mail. The devices are so addictive that they are sometimes called "CrackBerries." The manager allows guests to turn in their BlackBerrys to him so that they can learn to cope without them for a day or two while they enjoy whatever activities brought them to Chicago. He started the program because of his own problem. As he told Reuters, "I was really addicted to my BlackBerry. I had an obsession with e-mail. Morning and night. There came a time when I didn't think it was healthy. . . . I quit cold turkey."[1]

BlackBerrys are only one of many electronic devices that can lead to obsessive behavior. Video games can be even more addictive. In 2006 Europe's first detox clinic for video game addicts opened in Amsterdam. Keith Bakker, the director of the clinic, points out that video games can be just as addictive as gambling and drugs, and the addiction can be just as hard to get under control.[2] Some of the addicts are so hooked on the games that when they are going through treatment, they suffer withdrawal symptoms such as shaking and sweating when they see a computer.

One man, who started playing video games at age eight, was playing them for 14 hours a day by the time he went to college, and he started taking drugs so that he could stay alert enough to prolong his playing time. He told reporter Fia Curley, "For me, one joint would never be enough, or five minutes of gaming would never be enough. I would just keep going until I crashed out."[3] The addiction to video games, like addictions to other electronic devices, usually begins with the person thinking he or she will simply play for a few minutes before doing homework or other chores, but then a few minutes turns into half an hour, then an hour, then a whole evening or more. The person thinks, *just one more game, one more level,* just as the Internet-obsessed person thinks, *just one more Web site, just one more quick check of e-mail.*

CrazyBusy author Edward M. Hallowell has made up the word "gemmelsmerch" to describe "the ubiquitous force that distracts us from whatever we're doing." For instance, as you're watching television, do you ever have the irresistible urge to flip through the channels, even though you don't want to miss the show you're actually watching? And once you flip through the channels once, do you feel like doing it again, just in case you missed something or in case something better might be on? Hallowell writes, "In ages past, we might have wondered if something better was on, but we wouldn't have had three hundred channels to check out the possibility. A better job, a better book, a better restaurant, a better romantic partner—they are all there for our perusal much more immediately than ever before."[4]

So what's wrong with having so many choices? In the mid-1990s Dr. Hallowell noticed an increase in the number of patients coming to him feeling "chronically inattentive, disor-

ganized, and overbooked." Many thought they had Attention
Deficit Disorder (ADD), but most did not. Instead, they had
an "environmentally induced stand-in" with symptoms similar
to the real condition. The biggest problem with treating this
disorder is that many people don't *want* to get over it. Hallowell says, "No one needs to read three newspapers every day,
check e-mail every ten minutes, make or take scores of phone
calls every day, and channel surf during all conversations, tun-
ing out the moment stimulation subsides."[5] Then why do they
do it? Because it makes them feel charged up, part of the action and drama of life. For some, the fact they also feel frazzled and scattered is a price they are willing to pay.

As with the other kinds of noise we've discussed, it's easy to
dismiss this noise of the mind as simply an inevitable byprod-
uct of living in our fast-paced, technologically advanced culture. But it has an impact on everything about us. For instance, how does this psychologically noisy lifestyle affect how
we treat our family and friends? In one sense, the technology
might be seen as bringing people together, especially in the
cases described earlier of people who spend 10 or 12 hours a
day on their phones or sending Instant Messages.

However, the same technology can also isolate us. *Time*
magazine recently ran a cover story titled "Are Kids Too Wired
for Their Own Good?" The article begins by describing an
evening in the life of a Southern California family composed of
a mother, a father, a teenage boy, and a teenage girl: "By all
standard space-time calculations, the four members of the
family occupy the same home in Van Nuys, Calif., but psychologically each exists in his or her own little universe."[6] The son
spends the evening in his bedroom logged onto a chat room
and sending Instant Messages to friends. The daughter is in

another room sending Instant Messages, talking on her cell phone, and doing homework. The father is in a different room making business phone calls. The mother is alone in the living room tidying up. The family did not have dinner together.

Anthropologist Elinor Ochs leads a team of researchers studying modern family life. One thing they are looking at is what happens at the end of the day when parents and children come together. She told *Time,* "We saw that when the working parent comes through the door, the other spouse and the kids are so absorbed by what they're doing that they don't give the arriving parent the time of day." Most of the time the children do not greet the returning parent. She added, "We also saw how difficult it was for parents to penetrate the child's universe. We have so many videotapes of parents actually backing away, retreating from kids who are absorbed by whatever they're doing."[7]

Family relationships are not the only ones being harmed in this new era. According to the General Social Survey released in 2006, Americans in general are becoming more isolated. "A quarter of Americans say they have no one with whom they can discuss personal troubles, more than double the number who were similarly isolated in 1985," reported Shankar Vedantam in a *Washington Post* article on the survey. "Overall, the number of people Americans have in their closest circle of confidants has dropped from around three to about two."

This sense of isolation is growing even as the amount of time people spend communicating with each other online is increasing. Lynn Smith-Lovin, a sociologist who helped conduct the survey, said, "We're not saying people are completely isolated. They may have 600 friends on Facebook.com [a popular networking Web site] and e-mail 25 people a day, but they are not discussing matters that are personally important."[8]

What Spiritual Impact?

If all of our multitasking, Instant Messaging, channel-flipping, and other forms of psychological noise are keeping parents and children and friends apart, then is it possible that they might also be affecting another important Fatherly relationship, that of our relationship with our Heavenly Father? The problem is not that God cannot speak to us even when we're at our busiest and are stretched to the edge of our capabilities. If our relationship with Him is firmly grounded, He can be as close to us during those times as He is during our quiet times.

The real problem is that a noisy interior life *lures* us away from Him. In the clatter that fills our brain, our faith becomes merely one more item that we try to multitask. Jesus said, "Abide in me as I abide in you. Just as the branch cannot bear fruit by itself unless it abides in the vine, neither can you unless you abide in me" (John 15:4, NIV). If a noisy mind makes it hard to concentrate on work or even to sleep, then how much harder will that noise make it to achieve union with God? And when our thoughts are so fragmented and frazzled, will we even lose the *desire* to draw so close to Him? Will we continue to pay homage to Him, but only at about the same level of commitment that we devote to our favorite TV show or Web site? Abiding is the opposite of Instant Messaging. Will He be speaking—or waiting to speak—but we don't even hear Him?

It is possible to get the noise in our lives under control. Most of us won't even have to give up our Internet connections or cell phones to do so. But we can't afford to simply do nothing. In the next chapter we'll consider ways of quieting ourselves in order to better hear God's voice.

Questions for Reflection

1. Review the opening scene of this chapter. Do you have similar difficulty clearing away the distractions in order to enjoy times of deep concentration? What are the biggest distractions you face? Has this gotten better over the last few years, or worse? Why?

2. "Gemmelsmerch" is Dr. Edward Hallowell's term to describe "the ubiquitous force that distracts us from whatever we're doing." When you watch TV, for instance, you may have the irresistible urge to flip through the channels, even though you're enjoying the show you're actually watching. Something inside you is afraid you may be missing something on another channel. Is this phenomenon limited to TV watching, or does it also afflict us in other activities and relationships?

3. Video games, Blackberrys, television, and other devices can be not only time-consuming but also addictive. Do you feel yourself spending more time with any of these or other devices than you would like to? What makes them so appealing? What are the drawbacks and dangers of them? What, if anything, have you done to try to control the amount of time you spend with these things?

4. Americans are more isolated than ever, according to the General Social Survey highlighted in this chapter. One-fourth of them say they have no one with whom they can discuss personal troubles. Do you see evidence of that increased isolation? If so, what are the reasons for it?

5. "A noisy interior life *lures* us away from God. In the clatter that fills our brain, our faith becomes merely one more item that we try to multitask." Do you agree with this? If so, describe how this might play out in the life of an individual Christian.

5

REDUCING THE NOISE, CLUTTER, AND AGITATION THAT BLOCK GOD'S VOICE

I had to step away from my life for a few days before I fully understood how cluttered it is with the kinds of noise and distractions discussed in the previous chapter. The revelation occurred at a writers' retreat sponsored by my university. Unlike most academic retreats and conferences that I was used to, packed with workshops and presentations, this one began with only one motivational talk, followed by four days of free time to write, eat meals with fellow writers, and take walks on the beautiful grounds of a retreat center overlooking the Pacific Ocean. Compared to my usual routine, this sounded like paradise.

After the opening talk, I settled into my room to work. Our rooms had no televisions, telephones, or Internet access. I had no roommate. The place was quiet. I had my computer, a suitcase full of books and papers, and nothing scheduled until dinner.

I had no distractions to keep me from diving into my work, right?

Wrong. The one noisy device I could not turn down was my brain.

I began the previous chapter by describing a writing session ruined by distractions of every kind—phone messages, e-mails, Web sites, visitors at the door. Now most of those distractions were not even *possible,* but still my mind was too scattered to settle into my work. My first compulsion was to check my e-mail. That's how I normally began my writing sessions. I stared longingly at the icon that normally connected me to the Internet and that now was useless. I turned again to the writing and tried to focus.

My brain would not settle down. Maybe I should take a walk around the grounds first, I told myself. But no, it was too soon for a break. I hadn't done any work yet! That morning, before I left for the retreat, I had watched the news on television, and now as I sat at my computer not writing anything, snippets of those reports raced through my mind—the talking head political experts yelling at one another, their rapid-fire answers having nothing to do with the questions addressed to them. What would it be like to be cut off from news for four days, without even my morning paper to update me? I longed to jump onto the Internet just to get a quick update. What might happen while I was gone, with the wars and the natural disasters and the economy and the celebrity trials and the missing-persons stories and the crime stories and the weather reports? I usually told myself I wasn't a TV or news addict—I didn't really watch that much, but those stories, with their soap-opera-like suspense, kept me coming back for more. Now I was stranded in this room while the outside world might be going up in flames!

I stood up and paced around the room. It suddenly felt very tiny. I looked out the window, as if searching for evidence—maybe a thick black cloud in the distance—of the great world events I must be missing.

Maybe I should read for a while instead of trying to jump right into the writing. As I debated this with myself, I realized that, perhaps because of the drive to the retreat center or the hard work I had done in preparation for being able to go, I felt incredibly tired. I lay down on the bed and fell asleep for an hour.

When I woke up, I felt calmer. I went back to my computer, read through some notes, typed a few sentences. A few annoying little snippets of songs raced through my head. Fragments of TV commercials. Another desire to get online surged through me. I suppressed all this. I wrote a little more. I read, I looked through notes, I stared into the distance and let my thoughts take shape uninterrupted. I didn't hurry myself.

By the time dinner rolled around, *I had produced twice as much in that afternoon as I usually did in a normal workday at my office.* After a meal with friends and a walk to the ocean and back, I had more evening hours to write. At home this time of night would normally be filled with chores around the house, dinner with my wife and children, watching TV, playing with the kids, reading, and relaxing. Now, alone in my quiet room, my brain flared up again with its noise, but it was easier to calm the storm than it had been earlier in the day. After a good night's sleep, I had no trouble getting started again early the next day.

I had been at the retreat less than 24 hours, but already my mind was moving into a more sane, steady, productive state. Now each time I sat down at the computer, it was a little easier to turn down the volume of the clamor in my head and enter into the work. Entering this deeper, more tranquil frame of mind not only benefited my work but also made a difference in other ways I would not have expected. At work, lunches with my colleagues in the loud cafeteria were usually rushed, as people darted in to grab a quick meal before their next class. Conversations were often cut off in the middle of a thought, and the topics usually only skimmed the surface of what we really cared about. But here on the retreat, in the small dining room, people took their time to linger over meals. There was plenty of time to get back to the writing, so people slowed down and listened to each other. No one had to raise the volume in order to break through the usual chaos and rushed inattention.

Even my times of prayer, meditation, worship, and Scripture reading—there was plenty of time for these things!—broke through to a deeper level during those days. Instead of hurrying through the daily Scripture reading from my devotional guide and following up with a quick prayer, I instead could linger over the verses that stood out to me, as I listened for God's guidance in them. My times of prayer were different there in ways similar to how the mealtimes were different—beyond the content of the Scripture and prayer, there was the contentment of being in the presence of a true friend, someone with whom I was intimately connected. Prayer meant not only *speaking* to God but also *listening* to Him and feeling His love and reassurance that He cared for me and was leading me.

Most surprising of all was the impact this time away from the interior and exterior noise of my life had on me when I left the retreat and returned to the usual pandemonium down the mountain. Take my news addiction, for instance. As eager as I was at the beginning of the retreat to catch up on world events and the latest crime and celebrity stories, you might expect that after I got home from four days of a news blackout, I would rush to the TV news programs desperate to catch up.

In fact, I felt reluctant to let that noise back into my life. To my wife's surprise, I stopped watching TV news altogether for the next two or three months. The bombardment of photos and graphics and breathless reporters seemed too frantic and desperate. A daily update from my morning newspaper was plenty of information to keep me informed. I had discovered the pleasure of a mind uncluttered.

I also changed my attitude toward e-mail. Before the retreat, I had always begun my workday by checking e-mail, but now I realized how much more real work I had accomplished and how much clearer my thinking had been during those four days when I worked with my mind free of that steady barrage of messages. I set a new rule for myself that I not check e-mail or get on the Internet at all until the day's work was done.

Getting away from the noise for four days had readjusted my sense of what my normal state of mind should be. I had gotten so used to functioning with this constant mental onslaught that I had assumed that's how life has to be. Now I decided to see whether the chaos could be controlled.

Separating the Noisy Self from the Quiet Self

Here is a typical mealtime prayer at my house. My wife and I are trying to corral the kids and get them to sit down. There's always one more thing someone has to get from the refrigerator or cabinet. Multiple conversations are occurring simultaneously. Two or three of us may be ready to start, while one or two others may still be talking or moving around.

And that's when we pray.

Often, it is as short and perfunctory as we can make it. Maybe the voices and activities have stopped during the prayer, or maybe they haven't. Often, it is a mere ritual prelude to the meal rather than any genuine expression of gratitude toward the God from whom the blessing of this meal sprang. We say the prayer, it's over, we dig in.

Contrast that with my best times of prayer, those soul-searching times when God's presence settles over me, when I sense His guidance, feel His love and reassurance, learn from Him. These times happen only when the internal and external chaos of my life is quieted enough that I can open myself to hearing from Him.

I would not expect the mealtime prayer ever to be like that deeper time of prayer. Family mealtimes could never be turned into sessions that are primarily contemplative and reflective, nor would I want them to be. It's fun to have those lively hours together around the table. I believe God is pleased with our simple expression of gratitude.

The problem comes when almost *all* of our prayer life is as shallow as the mealtime prayer. Many Christians allow their entire spiritual lives to drift into this automatic mode. They go through the motions of attending church as habit dictates, praying according to tradition, reading the Bible or ignoring it as time permits, praying halfheartedly as the feeling strikes. It's not that these Christians *intend* to lead shallow spiritual lives, but it feels like that's all that circumstances allow. What can be done to break through to a deeper level?

Dr. Hallowell identifies a mind-set he calls the F-State, which can be defined by words such as "frenzied, feckless, flailing, fearful, forgetful, flustered, furious, fractious, feverish, and frantic." He contrasts that with what he calls the C-State of being "clear, calm, cool, collected, consistent, concentrated, convivial, careful, curious, creative, courteous, and coordinated."[1]

In his book, *In Praise of Slowness,* Carl Honore makes a distinction between what he calls fast thinking and slow thinking. He writes, "The spirit, by its very nature, is Slow. No matter how hard you try, you cannot accelerate enlightenment. Every religion teaches the need to slow down in order to connect with the self, with others and with a higher force."[2] British psychologist Guy Claxton has defined these two kinds of thinking in his book *Hare Brain, Tortoise Mind—Why Intelligence Increases When You Think Less.* As Honore explains it:

> Fast Thinking is rational, analytical, linear, logical. It is what we do under pressure, when the clock is ticking; it is the way computers think and the way the modern workplace operates; it delivers clear solutions to well-defined problems. Slow Thinking is intuitive, woolly and creative. It is what we do when the pressure is off, and we have the time to let ideas simmer at their own pace on the back burner. It yields rich and subtle insights.[3]

Our fast-paced workplaces, family lives, and even churches favor fast thinking over slow thinking, just as they push us closer to the F-State than the C-State. The answer to this imbalance is not to banish fast thinking from our lives. We need it. It helps us to function in the world and accomplish necessary tasks.

The key is balance. Can we learn to meet the demands of a turbulent world without losing our souls? Can we maintain serenity in the midst of chaos?

Although as a literature professor I teach the classics, some of my favorite books to read for pleasure are spy novels by writers such as John le Carré, Robert Littell, Graham Greene, and Charles McCarry. Many of these books portray men who operate successfully at the surface level in a bureaucratic world but who also have a secret self that functions at a deeper and more complex level. Although most of us are not spies and therefore have no need for actual separate identities, we do have a self that operates in the public, 9-to-5, task-oriented, chore-completing arena, and a slower, more thoughtful, quieter self that—if we don't squelch it—functions at a deeper level.

No labels are completely adequate to identify these levels or selves. We could speak of surface level/deep level, public self/private self, fast thinker/slow thinker, and so on, but none of those quite encompasses the idea. For the sake of this discussion, I have settled on the labels noisy self and quiet self to describe the two states of mind. Both of these selves have positive and negative characteristics.

On the positive side, the noisy self is task-oriented and able to complete many assignments. This self is able to multitask, enjoys the thrill of juggling lots of projects at once, and is actively involved with other people. This self likes to have fun and feels comfortable in big crowds and boisterous celebrations. On the negative side, the noisy self often feels irritable, pulled in too many directions. This self becomes impatient easily and is quick to anger over small difficulties or slights. The noisy self often feels bombarded by too many media voices, too many demands, too crowded a schedule. This self finds it hard to concentrate. The noisy self, having trouble quieting down internally, has a tendency toward rude behavior, such as speaking too loudly at inappropriate times and places like quiet restaurants, church services, and anyplace where a spirit of quiet contemplation is called for.

In contrast, one of the positive characteristics of the quiet self is the ability to approach life from a calm, "big picture" perspective and not get lost or overwhelmed by the frantic details of the moment. The quiet self enjoys creative bursts of ideas and is able to delve into those ideas with a sense of depth and complexity of thought. The quiet self is good at true, loving, one-on-one friendship. This self is drawn toward union with God and careful study of His Word. The quiet self is characterized by a sense of hope, contentment, and an awareness of life's small pleasures. On the negative side, the quiet self may at times be too reluctant to take action, preferring to sit on the sidelines and contemplate. This self may have difficulty handling the pace of other people's expectations and may feel left behind or inadequate in the face of rapidly changing technologies and practices. This self may have a tendency toward insularity, preferring the comfort of being alone or with a few trusted loved ones over the challenges of engaging with a hostile or competitive outside world.

Although it's possible to get our lives off-balance in either direction, for me, as well as for many people in our day, the quiet self is the easiest for me to neglect, not intentionally, but because of the pressures of everyday life in this noisy era. As someone who leads a "noisy" life of being a husband, father of two small children, professor, writer, cell phone user, e-mail fanatic, news junkie, and many other roles, I have found that there are ways of keeping my quiet self alive. Some of them are easy and some of them are hard.

I want to start with the easy ones. By "easy," I mean that you can accomplish them without great disruption to you or your family. They won't involve taking time off work or getting a babysitter or disrupting your responsibilities in ways that most people other than yourself will even notice. One way in which they may *not* be easy is that they may mean breaking free from long-established habits and compulsions. But doing these things may help bring you into that quieter, more receptive, more perceptive state in which you are truly able to listen to God and abide in His presence.

1. Don't check e-mail or other messages until as late in the day as possible

I put this one first because it has been more helpful to me than any other single lifestyle change I have made to maintain my quiet self in a noisy world. For me, the temptation is to *start* the day with e-mail, but if I do so, I can kiss concentration and deep creativity good-bye. E-mail scatters my thoughts in a dozen directions. It's as if a roomful of people are speaking to me at the same time, vying for my time and attention. I have to sort through it, put my mind on many different topics, decide which messages to answer now, which to answer later, and which to ignore. Even when I step away from it and try to get back to the work at hand, I find my mind wandering back to the messages, which makes me want to check it again to see if something else important might have arrived in my inbox.

The rule I have set for myself calls for waiting until 3 P.M. to check my messages. When I suggested this to a small group I was teaching on this issue, I heard gasps at the thought of waiting until so late in the day. Some said they absolutely could not do that because of the demands of their jobs. That may be true, and people have to adopt what works best for them, but the idea is to wait as late as possible before allowing that disruptive, concentration-breaking element into your life. One thing I reminded the group is that not all that long ago, e-mail didn't even exist, and people managed to live meaningful lives without it. Is it really so unreasonable to postpone it for several hours in order to maintain a more focused state of mind?

Following this rule was hard for me, especially at first. I felt antsy. I wondered what urgent message I must be missing. I tried to think of reasons to rationalize checking "just once." When 3 P.M. hit, I pounced on my messages like a thirsty man finding water in the desert. But now that this practice is fully established in my routine, I am no longer so frantic about it. I've learned that the messages can wait. And in the meantime, I can give focused attention to my work during the time of day when my mind is most productive.

2. Get more sleep

Just as many of us falsely tell ourselves that we can multi-task several chores without any real loss of effectiveness or concentration, we also fool ourselves into believing we really don't need a full night's sleep to function well. At the retreat that I told about at the beginning of this chapter, I mentioned that one of the first things I did as I tried to settle into my work in that quiet place was to fall asleep for an hour. I didn't plan that nap, nor was it a luxury I would have allowed myself during a normal workday. Many of us don't realize just how exhausted we are until we slow down for a moment.

In her book, *Invitation to Solitude and Silence,* Ruth Haley Barton writes that when you step away from your busy life and turn to solitude, "you may be surprised by what happens once you get to a place of silence. You may fall asleep while trying to pray. Perhaps you can't concentrate on the scripture you're reading. You may find yourself longing to curl up under a blanket and rest, and you try hard to resist your body's need."[4] Many people want to resist that urge to sleep, feeling guilty if they're not *doing* something to further their spiritual experience. You may try to ignore the tiredness and push yourself on. But if the exhaustion itself is what is keeping you from hearing God clearly, then resting—more than prayer or Scripture reading or any other activity—may be the most important first step you need to take to prepare you to enjoy His presence.

One of the most famous biblical stories of someone who fled into solitude and silence is that of Elijah, who sought refuge in the wilderness when Jezebel was trying to kill him. As Barton points out, God did not speak to the exhausted and discouraged Elijah as soon as he got out to the lonely place. First, he lay down under a broom tree and fell asleep. Barton writes, "God did not waste time trying to deal with him intellectually or even spiritually because it wouldn't have done any good. He began by dealing with Elijah's physical weariness and depletion—he let Elijah sleep. Then he woke Elijah up when it was time to eat and drink, provided food and water for him, told him to go back to sleep, and then started the process all over again."[5]

Exhaustion is often masked by the kinds of excessive, noisy activities already discussed. Honore points out that, "In the final stages before burnout, people often speed up to avoid confronting their unhappiness."[6] Barton makes a distinction between "good tired," which we experience as the result of an accomplished task, and "dangerous tired," which is a "chronic inner fatigue" that accumulates over many months. In her own life, she has learned that when she is dangerously tired, "I can be very, very busy and look very, very important but be unable to hear the quiet, sure voice of the One who calls me the beloved. When that happens I lose touch with that place in the center of my being where I know who I am in God, where I know what I am called to do, and where I am responsive to His voice above all others."[7]

We live in a world that values action over rest. But when we realize that exhaustion can be not only unproductive but also dangerous, we may also see that for the worn-out Christian, sleep itself can be a spiritual activity.

3. Cut out one television show or one hour of Internet time a day and spend that time in silence, meditative prayer, or Bible reading

One of the most common reasons people give for neglecting prayer, being alone with God, and regular Bible reading is, "I don't have time." Given our hectic lives, most of us could certainly make a strong case that we simply can't fit one more item on our daily agenda. However, it is also true for most of us that we have plenty of moments of the day that are wasted. By "wasted," I don't mean what is sometimes meant by that term, which is time that is not devoted to work or some other "productive" activity. As we've seen, many of us need *more* unstructured time to play with our kids, read a book for pleasure, sit on the porch and talk to neighbors, or linger at the dinner table after a meal to talk to our spouses.

By "wasted time," I am referring to those minutes and hours that slip away—even on our busiest days—and leave us vaguely unsatisfied, wondering where the time went. Nothing good is on television, but we find ourselves absently flipping through the channels anyway. An hour later, we're still flipping, having watched a little of this and a little of that, none of it worth our time. Or we check the news on one Web site, don't find much, so check another, then another, getting the same information over and over again, until we switch to something else that leaves us equally bored and antsy for something better.

What if we took one of those hours a day and set it aside for listening to God? I'm not talking about adding another burden to an already demanding schedule. I would not start with an ambitious program of trying to read through the Bible in a year or work through a long prayer request list or tackle a complex work of theology. The goal is to create an hour in your day that is spiritually refreshing, quiet, sane.

If you live with other people, ask your family to understand that you need this hour, and then close yourself off in a pleasant room where you can quiet your soul. One of the keys to making this time a regular part of your spiritual life is to do whatever you can to make it enjoyable. If it feels like a chore, you'll want to stop, and you'll easily find excuses to do so. But if it becomes one of the most fulfilling times of your day, as if it's a gift that you're giving to yourself, then you'll find yourself trying to think of ways to preserve it. Take a cup of coffee in with you, if you enjoy that, or a snack. You are going to spend time with a friend, so create the kind of atmosphere that friends would enjoy sharing. It may help to listen to some music that helps free your mind from the day's frantic pace.

At first, you may want to do nothing at all but let the music pour over you. Allow time for the noises of the day to quiet down inside your head. When you're ready, invite God to join you there. Invite Him with a simple prayer, such as, "Lord, I give you this hour to use as you see fit. I'm here to be with you. Please meet me here, Lord. I'm listening."

For some people, it may be helpful to read a short devotional or other book that helps bring you into God's presence. Or you might want to choose a favorite portion of Scripture to meditate on. The goal is not to get through a large chunk of text. That kind of Bible study is for another time, but right now the goal is to meditate on God's Word and invite Him to speak through it. For some, no text at all is necessary at this point. You simply enjoy the silence, or the music, and wait on God, listening for Him. You don't need to fill the space with lots of words, but simply *be there* to enjoy His presence, just as you enjoy being with any good friend regardless of the specifics of the conversation.

If you're used to a particularly hectic pace and a noisy lifestyle, then spending an hour might feel like a long time to spend on this kind of meditative activity at first. If so, then start with half an hour. Separating yourself even for a short time from the world of fragmented thoughts and endless demands in order to get in touch with God's presence will make this encounter with Him a joy. The next chapter will discuss prayer and Bible reading more in-depth, but this is an easy way to begin, and you may find that this time of communion with God becomes your favorite part of the day.

4. Walk or jog—quietly

Having walked several blocks from my home and warmed up, I take that first running step. I still feel a little stiff at first, but several paces later, the rhythm of the jog kicks in, as does the rhythm of my breathing, and I am off on my morning run. My route is familiar—four miles through a park, down a horse trail, across my neighborhood streets—so my mind is free to wander where it chooses. The rhythm slows down my thinking. Physically, the run is challenging, but in a good way, as I sweat, as my legs get tired, as I sometimes wonder whether I'll be able to finish the course today. But most of the time I don't think about the running at all. Free of distractions, I can concentrate on other things, do some of my best thinking of the day, pray, dream and plan for the future. When the run is over, I walk about half a mile back to my home to cool down. My mind and body feel confident, calm, ready for the challenges of the day.

If you're physically able to do so, walking or running regularly is an excellent way to reach your quieter self. The physical benefits are numerous, but it also gets you away from the noise of the day and opens up time and mental space for prayer and thought. To avoid interrupting that rhythm that can develop during walking or running, I would leave behind distractions like cell phones or music players. The outdoors, the exercise, and the serenity will be entertainment enough.

5. Review all your activities and commitments. If you find that your life is too noisy, decide on one activity that you can set aside in order to simplify your life

Most of our lives don't get noisy all at once, but the volume increases notch by notch while we're barely aware of it. When a new opportunity arises, we think, *Sure, why not? That sounds like a worthwhile thing to do. How much time could it possibly take?* We add it to our list of commitments. Although no individual obligation on our list seems too burdensome, we soon find our lives bogged down by an energy-draining weight of projects, committees, church activities, personal favors, work chores, hobbies, habits, entertainments, home improvement projects, and other pursuits.

If you are pulled in too many different directions because of an ever-increasing load of obligations, it may be time to assess all these activities and decide which one (or more) you can drop. You might begin by listing them on paper. Then ask, what are you involved in that is tangential to what your life is all about? What activity might once have served a purpose but now merely sucks time and energy from what you would rather be doing?

Making this move toward a simpler lifestyle is liberating, but doing it may not be as easy as it sounds. First, it may require you to disappoint people. You may have to quit or curtail your leadership in a group that has come to depend on you. They know you do a good job and will be hard to replace. They know you like being part of the group. It may not make sense to them that you are deciding to step away "only" because you need to simplify your life and this endeavor no longer fits your life's purpose.

Second, you may feel your own guilt for turning down an opportunity or stepping away from a position in which you have some interest and ability. For most of us, life offers far more opportunities than time and resources. Our inclination is to think that if we *can* do it and *want* to do it, that means we *should* do it. Only when we stop looking at these opportunities individually and instead ask how they fit into the tapestry of our lives as a whole will it make sense to say no to plans and projects that we are perfectly capable of fulfilling.

Third, simplifying your life may be a challenge in a culture in which "busy" most often equates to "successful" and "important." Our culture doesn't give much credit for achieving a well-balanced life or nurturing a more sane, quiet self that is attuned to God's Spirit. Simplifying your life may not make you look more important, but it will bring many other benefits. When your life has some space in it, for instance, you may be more open to soul-nurturing friendships and more loving relationships with family members. You won't so often feel the need to neglect time with family and friends in favor of the other obligations that, when you first agreed to them, seemed like no big deal. You may also open up room for listening to God rather than trying to squeeze Him in between activities or ignoring Him altogether.

6. Take time to enjoy the moment; draw attention to life's simple pleasures.

One of the biggest costs of a life that is too noisy is that the most joyful parts of life are the first to get drowned out. With demands pressing in from every side, you don't take time to notice the little pleasures of life—or even the big ones—because doing so doesn't help you work through your to-do list.

If you get the chance to drink a great cup of coffee or eat a delicious dessert, will you even pay attention enough to really taste it?

If you have a few minutes to play with your son or daughter, will you relish that time, or will you merely try to hide your restlessness because this play time is keeping you from something you really need to get done?

If a friend you haven't seen in a while stops into your office to say hello, will you welcome him as a pleasant surprise in your day, or will you hurry him along so you can get back to your work?

If the still, small voice of God speaks in the midst of your day, will you hear Him, or will the clamor that consumes your life block Him out?

Life is full of small pleasures, but instead of paying attention to them and living in the joy that could fill our lives, it is more natural for us to ignore those gifts and put our focus on whatever crises are at hand. We become full-time problem-solvers and chaos managers.

In my previous book, *When God Takes Too Long: Learning to Thrive During Life's Delays,* I have a chapter called "Embracing the Moment."[8] In it I talk about making a list of the good things that help me get through the day. These include everything from enjoying the first bites of a juicy, hot meal to playing handball with my son to giving my daughter a piggyback ride to enjoying my newspaper and cereal at breakfast. There are hundreds of these details, probably thousands, if I took the time to list them all. And yet on how many days do I allow myself to feel that life is made up primarily of burdens to be carried and tasks to be performed?

If you find that you're going through your days feeling harried and nitpicked, try making such a list. Add three or four items every day, and thank God for them. Before long, you'll wake up to the fact that despite your difficulties, God has filled your life with gifts to savor.

7. Set aside time to think

I used to feel guilty when my mind wanted to daydream as I worked in my office between classes. Now I schedule time for it.

Before I made that schedule change, I felt a sense of accomplishment at work only when I was *doing* something, which I defined as activity that led to a clearly visible outcome—a paper graded, an exam written, a message answered.

In the short run, task-completion feels more like work than Slow Thinking because finishing those individual chores allows me to put a check beside that item on the checklist and then move on to the next thing. But long-term, ignoring Slow Thinking as wasted or unproductive time cuts off the creativity needed for my best work.

I learned the value of setting aside time for thinking when I had a semester-long sabbatical from my university to write a book. I had all day to write, so one day I stopped my work and decided to give myself the luxury of taking a half an hour to do nothing but think. I didn't read or write notes or do any other chore. I looked out the window and thought. What about? Anything that came to mind. I let my mind wander, pleasantly daydreaming from one idea to another. I considered it time *away* from work, but it ended up feeding the work. Some of my best ideas came during that half-hour, which benefited my writing for the rest of the day. From then on, I scheduled free time for thinking each day.

Even some business leaders have learned the value of giving their employees time to think. They've discovered that pushing workers harder simply to *do* more and work faster can be counterproductive. Management professor Peter Capelli said, "On the organizational level, what you get is, everyone is so focused on running flat-out to meet current goals that the whole company is unable to step back and think."[9] Emphasizing only immediate tasks keeps a person stuck in old ways of thinking. As business expert Peter Drucker put it, "All one can think and do in a short time is to think what one already knows and to do as one has always done."[10] Actually *scheduling* time to think may free you from the pressure or guilt you might otherwise feel to get back to work. During your thinking time, be sure to keep yourself away from distractions like books, magazines, computers, and phones, and then let your mind roam free.

8. Do one thing a day to unclutter the space in which you live and work

Clutter is a type of noise, and a working or living space that is too disorderly may contribute to your feeling bogged down and out of control. Dr. Hallowell writes, "I have seen people reduced to tears as they tell me of the clutter that fills their offices. They have even brought me photos to prove their point. . . . When I ask them the obvious questions like 'Why don't you set aside time to clean your office or hire someone else to do it for you?' they look at me as if I were a child, oblivious to the advanced nature of their disease."[11]

Clutter can seem so overwhelming that we feel hopeless in the face of it. The best approach to getting it under control may be to not try to eliminate it all at once. Instead, try un-cluttering one small area a day. Clean off the top of a file cabinet, for instance, throwing away anything you don't need and putting the rest of it where it belongs. The next day, choose another small space to conquer. The work involved to do this will be minimal, but the cluttered feel will diminish surprisingly quickly. Start with the space you spend the most time in and work out from there. The idea is not to become super-organized or spotless. Creating more space in your physical environment may be liberating in ways similar to how the other suggestions in this chapter create space in your mental and spiritual environment.

9. When driving alone, make your car a sanctuary of solitude and prayer

I've been surprised by how many Christians I have talked to who say their best times of prayer happen in their cars when they're commuting to and from work or taking some other lengthy trip alone. I know people who deliberately leave the radio off when they're alone in the car so they can use the time to pray and think. The confined space, the relative quiet, the monotony of the traffic, and the lack of distractions make the car an ideal place of quiet reflection for many people.

10. Serve others

At first, serving others may sound like a strange way to quiet yourself enough to hear God's voice in your life. In fact, it may seem to contradict that desire, since serving others may complicate your life rather than simplify it. However, if you have been involved with reaching out to others and pouring your life into theirs—in any of the thousands of ways this can be done—you know that getting the focus off yourself can transform your relationship to God.

Jesus calls us to love one another. Serving others releases love in our lives in ways that open doors to God's presence. He often draws close to us *as* we serve, and He sometimes speaks to us *through* those we serve, whether it's a child we're teaching in Vacation Bible School or a neighbor who needs our help with a project or a friend who needs someone to listen.

Any of these 10 suggestions are steps you can start right away. You may want to choose the one that seems easiest, try it for a week, and then add another.

For some, these steps may be enough, but others might want to explore even deeper ways of using silence, spiritual retreats, prayer, and Bible reading to draw closer to God, which we will look at in the next chapter.

Questions for Reflection

1. After considering the 10 ideas for reaching a quieter state of mind presented in this chapter, which steps do you think would be easiest for you to incorporate into your life right away? Which would be hardest?

2. Do you agree that clutter is a type of noise? How does a cluttered work space or living area affect you? What ways have you found to reduce clutter?

3. Have you found your car to be a good place of prayer? How might you best make spiritual use of your time alone in the car?

4. Does the final suggestion, "Serve others," really fit in this list? What does your own experience suggest about the impact that service has on your state of mind?

6

FINDING GOD IN THE SILENCE

As you pull your car into your church parking lot, a drain-ing weariness settles over your spirit. You wish you could turn around and drive away to almost anywhere—a coffee shop, back home to the TV or newspaper, even to work. You go through the motions of smiling and greeting people, but as you take your place in the sanctuary and scan the congrega-tion, you find more to criticize than to enjoy. Your attention locks on those who irritate you, those you consider judgmen-tal or hypocritical or simply bothersome. The service itself feels too long, filled with too much verbiage, too many half-baked ideas. You want to flee. For you, this entire exercise is void of God's presence. It's been a long time since you've sensed Him in this church or much of anywhere else. You feel a nagging doubt about all you have believed, a vague disap-pointment in God, a longing for a spiritual reality you can't even identify.

The symptoms of spiritual burnout vary for different peo-ple, but if the scenario described above sounds familiar to you, then you may be in it. Although painful and bewildering, this state of mind may, if you let it, be a door that will open in-to a deeper, life-giving experience of solitude and communion with God. How can you get there? In the previous chapter we looked at some ways to reduce the noise level of our lives in order to hear God's voice. Those ideas are a good place to start, but if you are in a deeper spiritual crisis, those may not be enough. The answer may lie in a deeper commitment to solitude, silence, and prayer.

Some assume that, given their busy lifestyles, solitude could never find a significant place in their lives. Surely the cost would be too high. But the busy people whose stories we will look at in this chapter have found that this is not true. Solitude and silence are not only for a chosen few. They are not only for those who abandon jobs and responsibilities to spend time alone with God. The methods vary widely, but anyone can practice them. The hard part is making the commitment to move forward. *The key is not to let your hesitation over finding exactly the right method keep you from beginning*. This chapter will look at ways that people have managed to do it.

Planning a Spiritual Retreat—for an Hour, a Day, a Week, or a Year

For some Christians, retreats become so important they can't imagine their spiritual lives without them. Robert Benson wrote, "Twenty-one weeks is the absolute maximum amount of time that I can go without some meaningful silence and solitude, or else my nerves get shaky, my work suffers, and my relationships start running on empty. That period of roughly one hundred and fifty days is about fifty percent farther than I should attempt to travel without a retreat."[1]

People adopt a variety of patterns for spiritual retreats. Some choose retreats that are completely silent. Some set aside not just a day but a week or more. Some follow a more formal or liturgical pattern. Some exclude any outside distractions or reading material, including the Bible. Worrying too much about the exact format of the retreat may become an excuse that keeps you from making *any* kind of soul-changing move into solitude. It may be better to enter into God's presence in a short afternoon retreat than to do nothing while you wait for the perfect time and format to emerge for a weeklong time at the ideal retreat center. With that in mind, here are some issues to consider as you plan a spiritual retreat.

Timing

How long should a personal retreat last? Jane Rubietta, in her book *Resting Place: A Personal Guide to Spiritual Retreats,* offers a plan for a retreat that might last a day or two. She believes that even a retreat that lasts only for an afternoon can be beneficial. You can plan this time at a retreat center if one is available to you, but she says even a state park or a friend's home or any other place where you can be alone and undistracted will work fine. Her book includes tools to use during the retreat, such as quotations to contemplate, scripture verses to meditate on, questions to write journal entries about, and hymns to sing.[2]

Most people I've talked to who do spiritual retreats plan them to last one day. Every few years, when they can manage it and when they feel a particular need for a longer time of solitude, they may take a retreat that lasts a week or more. If you've never done a personal retreat before, then a day might be long enough the first time around. One thing to keep in mind is that it takes time to move from the frantic everyday world into a time of solitude. My friend Laura, who has taken regular personal retreats for years, said, "For me, I am always reminded of how long it takes to get still before God. Often people find there is a period of squirming, distraction, taking a long time to get settled, before God breaks through and they are calm enough to hear from God."

Laura used to do her one-day retreats at a Benedictine monastery outside Los Angeles. She said, "Benedictines are known for their hospitality and for prayer (they pray several times each day). I usually would try to get there for morning prayers ("Lauds") and spend most of my day in a quiet garden there, reading and journaling (or hiking and praying around the grounds) and then join them for Vespers before dinner." She sometimes found that the quiet of the place brought out a burst of creative energy in her, and she spent part of the day drawing and writing poetry—two activities she never does otherwise—and taking photographs. Now that she lives in Oregon, she has switched her retreats to the coast, where she rents a beach house from a friend and spends her time collecting rocks, singing Christian music, sleeping, staring into the fire, journaling, reading, and praying.

No matter how you decide to structure your retreat, one thing to avoid is making it a time to catch up on work. That defeats the whole purpose of a "retreat" from the everyday noise of life. My friend Dick, who takes occasional spiritual retreats, said, "I have to guard against making this just another 'activity time' since there is a proneness to want to be 'productive.' It is difficult to disengage from such a high-paced, communication-driven, activity-addictive world, but it must happen." The core of his time away is centered on "deliberate silence (around and in me) and other spiritual disciplines such as prayer, reading, fasting, and simplicity."

Even if you feel you can't yet arrange or are not yet ready for a day-long retreat, don't overlook the value of including a much shorter daily time of solitude into your schedule. When Ruth Haley Barton began her journey into solitude, she started with 10 minutes of silence each day. She said, "While 'normal' students get to start out with 20 minutes of silence, I needed to begin with a more modest goal of 10 minutes a day because that was all I could handle. But no matter; I decided it was better to celebrate small successes than become discouraged by larger failures."[3]

Barton has straightforward advice for how to enter into a practice of solitude and silence. First, create a sacred *space*, a place set aside specifically for these times alone with God. Next, create a sacred *time* for giving God your undivided attention. No other work—even spiritual work like planning a Sunday School lesson—will be allowed into this time that is for God alone. Also, set a reasonable *amount* of time to spend in silence and prayer. When you begin, start with a simple prayer that opens you to listening to God. Her own phrase is, "Here I am." She suggests a word or phrase of just a few syllables, which you can repeat throughout your time whenever distractions arise. The focus is not on wordy prayers, but rather on listening for God and inviting Him in. Finally, end your time with a prayer of gratitude to God for meeting you there.[4]

Some Further Thoughts on Prayer and Meditation During Solitude

Regardless of whether your time of silence lasts for 20 minutes a day or for a week or more during a silent retreat, you will probably want to spend much of that time in meditation and prayer. If you are not used to times alone with God, you may find this daunting, since you don't even know *how* to fill so many hours in prayer.

One movement that Christian thinkers and writers such as Henri J. M. Nouwen, Thomas Merton, and Kenneth Leech use as a model of how prayer should be practiced is a group known as the Desert Fathers, who lived in the Egyptian desert in the fourth and fifth centuries. Just as Barton stays away from wordy prayers in her own daily times of solitude, beginning with the simple phrase, "Here I am," the Desert Fathers had a very similar idea. Nouwen explains:

> A word or sentence repeated frequently can help us to concentrate, to move the center, to create an inner stillness and thus to listen to the voice of God. When we simply try to sit silently and wait for God to speak to us, we find ourselves bombarded with endless conflicting thoughts and ideas. But when we use a very simple sentence, such as "O God, come to my assistance," or "Jesus, master, have mercy on me," or a word such as "Lord" or "Jesus," it is easier to let the many distractions pass by without being misled by them.[5]

Rather than being a time of *presenting* lots of words and requests to God, which is how we sometimes think of prayer, the prayer of these times of solitude may be much more about *listening* to God, moving to a deeper and quieter spiritual place where we can abide with Him. Instead of trying to bring Him into alignment with our plans, dreams, and ambitions, we instead set aside our own agendas and bask in His love and guidance. Kenneth Leech, also drawing on the experiences of the Desert Fathers and others, writes that a desert spirituality is about simplicity and waiting: "Our desert times then will be marked by the prayer of simple waiting, empty-handed, open to the moving of the Spirit. But this means that we must cultivate a silent, reflective spirit, uncluttered by distraction, calm, trustful, prepared for darkness and the wasteland. Our prayer will be very largely wordless, a vigilant state of abiding, of seeking, in peace and dark faith, to discern the signs of God's activity, yet prepared to wait without sign."[6]

An Approach to Meditating on Scripture During Silent Times

You may spend part of your time during a spiritual retreat or daily time of solitude delving into the Bible, since that is one of the most powerful ways God speaks to us. What is the best way to approach the Bible during a retreat or other time of solitude? Should you just start reading and try to get through as much as possible? Should you choose one portion of the text, gather commentaries, compare translations, and try to understand that part of Scripture as thoroughly as possible?

These and other ways of studying Scripture may have their place depending on how much time you have and what your goals are in understanding the Bible, but one of the methods that works best for times of solitude and retreat is one that Dallas Willard outlines in *Hearing God*. Drawing from a 17th-century book by Madame Guyon, Willard suggests beginning with portions of Scripture that are familiar to us, such as Rom. 8 or Ps. 23. The goal of this method is not simply to understand the passages at a level of scholarly knowledge, though that may be a worthy goal in other contexts. In this approach to Scripture, your desire is to move these passages of Scripture into the very substance of your life. You desire that God will meet with you and speak to you through these powerful words. You will not make rapid progress through the books of the Bible this way. You won't read through the Bible in a year—a type of study that you may want to do separate from this—but the passages you do study will be firmly ingrained in you in a deep and life-changing way.

Once you choose your biblical passage, you meditate on it in five steps, which include *information* about the passage, *longing* for it to be so, *affirmation* that it *must* be so, *invoca-*

tion to God to make it so, and *appropriation* by God's grace that it *is* so. What follows is how Willard demonstrates the process with Ps. 23:1, *The LORD is my shepherd, I shall not want.*

> First, you will find *information,* which you may not automatically transfer to yourself. You may say, "This was true just for David, the psalmist." But as you dwell prayerfully on the plain information, a *yearning* that it might be so for *you* may arise. You may express this, saying, "I wish the Lord were my shepherd; that the great God would have for me the care and attention that the shepherd has for his sheep!" And as you meditate on the psalm, *affirmation* may arise, as it has for so many people ("It must be so! I will have it be so!") followed then perhaps by *invocation* ("Lord, make it so for me") and *appropriation* (the settled conviction that it is so, that it is a statement of fact about you.)[7]

These steps are only tools and don't need to be approached in a narrow or legalistic way. There are other ways to bring the Bible deeply into your life, but if you are uncertain how to begin, this method might be a place to start.

For those who find it helpful to have more structure in their prayer and Bible reading, another useful approach is outlined in Mark A. Moore's book *The Rhythm of Prayer: A Forty Day Experience.*[8] His book offers a daily liturgy that consists of directed prayers, scripture selections, and times of reflection and silence.

You may find that other books in addition to the Bible may be inspiring and helpful during your times of solitude. The list of possibilities could go on for pages, but you may want to delve into the works of writers like C. S. Lewis, St. John of the Cross, Dietrich Bonhoeffer, Phillip Yancey, and many others.

Get recommendations from trusted Christian friends, and ask God to guide you to those books you need the most.

Solitude Is a Place of Spiritual Battle

In the clamorous and chaotic world in which we live, it may be tempting to use our times of solitude merely as times of escape. We might think of them as rare opportunities to get away from people who demand too much of us, work that saps our energy, distractions that drive us crazy, chores that wear us down. In our retreat or our daily time of solitude, we can be free to daydream, rehearse the hurtful words spoken to us throughout the day, think up responses we wish we had said, and think how glad we are not to have to deal with those everyday problems for a while.

A temporary escape from noise may have some therapeutic value in itself, but spiritual solitude is about much more. As Nouwen puts it: "If solitude were primarily an escape from a busy job, and silence primarily an escape from a noisy milieu, they could easily become very self-centered forms of asceticism. But solitude and silence are for prayer. The Desert Fathers did not think of solitude as being alone, but as being alone with God. They did not think of silence as not speaking, but as listening to God. Solitude and silence are the context within which prayer is practiced."[9]

Far from being comforting, our move into solitude at first may be difficult and disturbing. Part of the function of noise in our lives is to keep us distracted from who we truly are. When that protective layer of chaos is stripped away and we find ourselves alone before God, we may not like the self who confronts us there. In the scary silence, our first impulse may be to scurry back to the shields we normally rely on throughout our day to keep our true selves from being revealed—our busyness, our professional or familial roles, our credentials, our accomplishments, our excuses, our ambitions, our TV shows, our phone calls. Who are we when we are alone before God, without all those things to rely on? Here is how Nouwen describes the sometimes distressing initial movement into solitude:

As soon as I decide to stay in my solitude, confusing ideas, disturbing images, wild fantasies, and weird associations jump about in my mind like monkeys in a banana tree. Anger and greed begin to show their ugly faces. I give long, hostile speeches to my enemies and dream lustful dreams in which I am wealthy, influential, and very attractive—or poor, ugly, and in need of immediate consolation. Thus I try again to run from the dark abyss of my nothingness and restore my false self in all its vain glory.[10]

That is not exactly the consoling, relaxing image of solitude we often have. Leech warns, "To go straight from a world of ceaseless activism into total, uninterrupted solitude can be frightening, and we need to be prepared for panic."[11] The "desert," he says, "is initially a negative encounter; it is the place where illusions are smashed, the place of stripping, of unmasking, of purgation. It is therefore inevitably a place of great pain and upheaval. It is also the place of discovery of that central solitude which exists at the core of each of us."[12]

How can we survive this initial stage of dread and discomfort long enough to allow solitude to do its good work in us? Leech suggests that we may need a "soul friend" or spiritual companion or guide to reassure us during this early period, encouraging us that we are safe and whole and moving closer to God. Nouwen stresses the importance of *perseverance:* "The task is to persevere in my solitude, to stay in my cell until all my seductive visitors get tired of pounding on my door and leave me alone." He is quick to point out, however, that we cannot win this struggle in our own strength. "Anyone who wants to fight his demons with his own weapons is a fool. The wisdom of the desert is that the confrontation with our own frightening nothingness forces us to surrender ourselves totally and unconditionally to the Lord Jesus Christ."[13]

What Difference Will the Spiritual Retreat Make?

What should we expect from a spiritual retreat? How might it change us? One thing to keep in mind is that each retreat may serve a different purpose and bring about a different result. Sometimes the times of deep prayer, solitude, and thinking may lead to specific guidance about where your life is headed, what your next steps should be, where you should put your priorities.

At other times, however, your time alone with God may lead to something less specific but just as powerful. You may come to know, in a way that you had forgotten in the midst of the noise of your life, how deeply God loves you. His powerful Spirit at work in you helps you to understand that, beyond any circumstances, He is present with you and is working toward your ultimate good. You may have entered your retreat feeling bogged down and carrying an oppressed spirit of being stretched too thin, overworked, on the verge of illness or exhaustion. Encountering God in solitude may allow you to leave your time alone with Him cut loose from those chains. You are able to enter your noisy world in a quieter, more settled frame of mind that will be able to better withstand the buffeting demands of life. Your perspective of the circumstances of your life has broadened, and you are better able to sense God's presence and hear His voice.

Here is how Barton describes the place that solitude can take us: "Beyond formulaic approaches designed to harness God for our purposes, we learn to relinquish control and simply be present to the one whose presence is the bedrock of our being. Given time, we experience that loving presence as our ultimate reality. We learn in the very cells of our being that this reality never changes; it is only our awareness of it is sometimes dulled by the noise and clutter of life."[14]

If silence and solitude are doing their real work in us, and we are communing with God at a deeper level during these times alone with Him, then we can expect these encounters to change us once we are with people again. The world outside us may be just as chaotic as it was before, but we are changed. Because our own inner turmoil has been reduced, we are able to look at those around us with a fresh and more loving perspective. Our irritation threshold has been raised. A harsh word or rude action that might have sparked our immediate backlash before now is easier to absorb. It's not that we have achieved a serenity that will remain unbroken in all situations, but we become less prone to overreact, and we see the world with more generous, less cynical eyes.

Through her own practice of silence and solitude, Barton discovered that much of what happens during those times "ends up being 'for others'—as paradoxical as that sounds," and the change starts with our way of speaking to others:

> Our speech patterns are refined by the discipline of silence, because growing self-awareness enables us to choose more truly the words we say. Rather than speech that issues from subconscious needs to impress, to put oth-

ers in their place, to compete, to control and manipulate, to repay hurt with hurt, we now notice our inner dynamics and choose to speak from a different place, a place of love, trust and true wisdom that God is cultivating within us.[15]

Our family members and others in our lives sometimes have to make sacrifices when we take time for solitude and silence, as we temporarily turn over some of our responsibilities to them or postpone chores that otherwise would have filled our time. They may resist or resent our taking this time away if they believe it is nothing more than an extended coffee break or a selfish little vacation away from them. But if they see that the fruit of these times is that we are better, more loving, more compassionate people when we are with them, they may be more likely to want to encourage us to continue this important discipline in our spiritual journey.

Jesus himself struggled, persevered, and sought connection with the Father through solitude. What can we learn from the way He used silence during His days on earth?

The Crowds Seek Jesus; Jesus Seeks Solitude

When you think of how short a time Jesus' few years of earthly ministry were in the scheme of thousands of years of human history, you might imagine that He would want to spend almost every minute of that time reaching out to people, performing miracles, teaching, and preaching. The world would experience Him this way only briefly, so shouldn't He touch as many people as possible? Yet the Gospels are full of incidents in which Jesus sneaks off for time alone to pray. He knew that in spite of the many demands on Him, He needed time for communing with the Father, and He went to great lengths to find it.

If anyone had the right to use the excuse, "I'm too busy for silent time with God," Jesus did, but He made time for solitude even when it caused His disciples and others inconvenience and distress. Jesus' miraculous healing power alone made Him so in demand that He could have spent every minute of every day curing people. Luke 5:15 says, "But now more than ever the word about Jesus spread abroad; many crowds would gather to hear him and to be cured of their diseases." Meeting their needs sounds like a great way for Jesus to have spent His time, but the next verse says, "But he would withdraw to deserted places and pray." Jesus knew what many of us forget, that His powerful healing and teaching that happened during His times among the crowds depended upon His close connection with the Father that was nurtured when He was alone.

Even when His own disciples were panic-stricken on a boat during a storm they believed was going to kill them, where was Jesus? On a mountain alone, praying, having sent them off in the boat and having sent the crowds away (Matt. 14:22-33). He walked out on the water and saved them, just as He always broke away from times of solitude to go back to the people who needed Him. He never used solitude as an excuse to neglect the *action* that He needed to perform in His ministry, but He never allowed circumstances to squeeze prayer out of His life.

Many of us do not turn to solitude until we feel desperate, exhausted, or stretched to our breaking point, but Jesus didn't wait until things fell apart to enter into times of silence. In fact, He sometimes surprised His disciples by stealing away at moments of His greatest triumph and highest popularity. In Mark 1:33, for example, "The whole city was gathered around the door" of Simon's house as Jesus healed many sick people and cast out demons. Instead of staying there to bask in popularity or to attract an even larger group the next day, "In the morning, while it was still very dark, he got up and went out to a deserted place, and there he prayed. And Simon and his companions hunted for him. When they found him, they said to him, 'Everyone is searching for you'" (vv. 35-37). Having prayed, He now knew that it was time to move on to the other towns to proclaim His message.

Jesus' times of silence with the Father kept Him centered, grounded. He would not let himself be sidetracked by other people's expectations. Right after the miraculous feeding of the five thousand in John 6, the people began to say, "This is indeed the prophet who is come into the world" (John 6:14). It would have been easy for many of us to have gotten swept up in the enthusiasm of the crowd at that point, but "when Jesus realized that they were about to come and take him by force to make him king, he withdrew again to the mountain by himself" (v. 15).

Earlier in this chapter we examined the idea that times of solitude are often more about spiritual battle than they are about spiritual relaxation. This was true in Jesus' experience as well. Jesus spent 40 days fasting and being tempted by the devil in the desert in Luke 4 near the beginning of His ministry. Near the end of His ministry, He spent an agonizing night praying to the Father at Gethsemane (Matt. 26:36-46). Though both of these were severe times of trial in which the temptation to flee to a safer place must have been strong, Jesus did not flinch in either case. He fought the spiritual battle alone with the Father and won, despite the pain.

So far we have considered the ways in which the noise of our lives can drown out God's voice, and we have examined practices of silence, solitude, and prayer that may draw us closer to Him and be more attuned to His Spirit. Even when we consistently practice these disciplines, however, there are times in our lives when it still seems that God goes silent. These times can be frightening, bewildering, and discouraging. They can also be periods of significant spiritual growth if we do not cut short the process. The following chapters will examine what may happen to us during times of God's silence.

Questions for Reflection

1. On a sheet of paper, brainstorm ideas for a day-long or afternoon-long spiritual retreat, using ideas from this chapter. What steps can you take to make this plan a reality?

2. What are the biggest obstacles that stand in the way of your taking time out for solitude with God? Is finding the time the hardest part? Are you worried that you won't know how to best use the time or will be too restless to enjoy it? How can those difficulties be overcome?

3. As you consider Jesus' approach to solitude and silence, is there anything He did that surprises you? What can you learn from His example?

7

MISINTERPRETING GOD'S SILENCE

A girl named Amy is attracted to a boy named Brandon in her high school. For weeks she has seen him from a distance, and finally she and her friends find a way to "accidentally" run into him in the cafeteria at lunch. He shows interest in her, and the next day he comes up and talks to her on his own. After a couple more lunchtime encounters, he promises to call her on her cell phone that evening. She's thrilled, and she goes home that day waiting for the phone to ring.

The phone stays silent.

She keeps pulling the phone out and looking at it, willing it to ring. Brandon didn't say exactly when he would call, but when dinner rolls around and the call still hasn't come, she slinks off to her room, trying to hide from her family that sinking feeling that has settled over her.

She doesn't want to make the promise of this phone call the center of her life, but she can't help glancing at the phone repeatedly as she does her homework. An hour of silence goes by. She puts the phone on the other side of the room and vows to put it out of her mind.

Ten minutes later, it rings! She leaps for the phone. She calms her breathing, wanting to sound as if she had forgotten the call altogether and was absorbed in something else. "Hello?"

"Has he called yet?"

It's her best friend Natalie. Amy can't hide the disappointment from her voice.

A few more agonizing silent hours go by before bedtime. Brandon has let her down. She doesn't have his phone number and can't think of anyone who could get it for her.

By the time she arrives at school the next morning, she is hopeful again, thinking maybe Brandon will explain his failure to call and will make up for it with a tender apology.

He's not at school! Where is he? No one seems to know.

That night, with the phone still silent and her questions still unanswered, her feelings swing wildly from despair to hope to anger. How should she interpret his silence? She makes a mental list of the possibilities:

• Was he merely leading her on and had no intention to call?

• Was he too shy to call?

• Did he pick up the phone 10 or 12 times but then put it back down because he was afraid he'd say the wrong thing and blow his chances with her?

• Has he been too busy to call? Was he waiting until he had plenty of time so that the call wouldn't have to be rushed?

• Did he lose her phone number?

• Does he already have another girlfriend that he called instead?

• Has some horrible accident *prevented* him from calling?

• Was he abducted by aliens?

• Was he merely a figment of her imagination, and he never promised to call her in the first place?

The truth is that *she simply doesn't know* why he hasn't called, and all the speculation and worry in the world won't get her any closer to the truth. She will have to wait for the facts, and then she will know. If she settles on any particular explanation too quickly, she is likely to be dead wrong.

Nothing is as easy to misinterpret as silence. If you don't believe that, take a few minutes to think of some times when someone has misinterpreted your own silence. Have you ever been accused of pouting or being angry when in fact you were merely deep in thought or tired? Has someone ever taken your silence to mean approval when it really meant skepticism? Has someone ever interpreted your silence as disapproval when it really meant satisfaction or shyness?

As Christians, even when we are practicing the kinds of spiritual disciplines like solitude and prayer discussed in the previous chapters, most of us will experience times in our lives when God goes silent. For reasons unknown to us, we feel the pain of the withdrawal of His presence. Our spiritual lives go cold. Not understanding what is happening, we may panic. We may rebel. We may sink into discouragement. Tragically, we may misinterpret God's silence and give up on Him altogether.

That doesn't have to happen. As strange as it may sound, God may be doing some of His most significant spiritual work in us during those dry times. How can we cling to our faith and let the silence do its work? How can we avoid the trap of misconstruing God's silence?

God's Silence Does Not Mean He Is Abandoning or Punishing Us

As an author, I don't have personal contact with most of the people who read my books. It's encouraging when I get e-mails and letters from some of them, but I know that the vast majority will never write. As a reader, I do not have personal contact with most of the authors who are important to me. I never write letters to those authors. In fact, most of them are dead. This physical separation between author and reader does not mean, however, that significant and even life-changing communication is not taking place. There are a few long-dead authors who I feel I know even better than I know some of the people I see every day. If an author assumed that the reader's silence meant that the reader was not there or was not interested in the book, he would be misinterpreting the truth about the reader. The reader *is* there. The reader *is* responding to the work.

Much of the time our impressions of God—our sensing of His Spirit—can give us a good indication of our relationship with Him. As Rom. 8:16 puts it, "The Spirit himself testifies with our spirit that we are God's children" (NIV). However, even in times when we don't sense God's Spirit, that doesn't mean God isn't there. This loss of the sense of His Spirit can come about for a number of reasons. One reason we feel separated from Him may be that we are engaged in sinful practices that are blocking the relationship. In that case, we need to turn to Him in repentance to seek forgiveness. But even when we are following Him as best we know how, His Spirit may still seem distant. Tragedy may shake our faith. Long-term disappointments may wear us down. We may get so exhausted that we reach a point of spiritual burnout. Sometimes there is no particular cause of this spiritual dryness that we can identify.

During those times when God is silent, sometimes all we can cling to is our *knowledge* and our *faith*—rather than our *impression*—that He is still there and that, though silent, He will never leave us. We take refuge in Heb. 13:5, which says, "God has said, 'Never will I leave you; never will I forsake you'" (NIV). Jerry Bridges writes about this verse, "The Puritan preacher Thomas Lye remarked that in this passage the Greek has five negatives and may thus be rendered, 'I will not, not leave thee; neither will I not, not forsake thee.' Five times God emphasized to us that He will not forsake us. He wants us to firmly grasp the truth that whatever circumstances may indicate, we must believe, on the basis of His promise, that He has not forsaken us or left us to the mercy of those circumstances."[1] When we are at our lowest points spiritually, there are times when a promise from the Bible will sound like mere words and will offer little comfort. On the other hand, I have known times when, even though I was so discouraged by God's absence that I was on the verge of quitting the Christian life, deep within me was a core of belief that this verse must be true, and God must still be there, if only I would hold on.

Plunged into Silence, Crying Out to God

One of the periods of my life in which I felt the pain of God's silence most acutely was a time in which I also had to endure the hurtful silence of other people. It began not long after my wife and I got married, when we decided to have children.

Like so many couples, when we first got married we had taken the ability to have children for granted. We scheduled it into our lives in the same way we made our plans to buy a home or fund a retirement plan. Then came months of fruit-less waiting. That was followed by infertility discussions with doctors, medicines that didn't work, surgery, more waiting, and finally a doctor's blunt opinion that we would almost certainly never have children.

Disappointed but not ready to give up on parenthood, we looked into adoption. We prayed about it. We felt led to pursue it. After investigating the various ways of adopting, we hired an adoption attorney and prepared the portfolio of photos and information about ourselves that were given to birth mothers who were planning to put their babies up for adoption. Then came another year and a half of waiting. This phase contained its own deflating moments. Our hopes would rise when a birth mother would call to interview us, but then we would find out that we were only one of seven or eight other couples she was considering. When she chose someone else, we felt the same crush of disappointment that had hit us with every other failed attempt to have children. Why weren't we chosen? What was wrong with us? The lawyer told us not to worry. Birth mothers, she said, often chose couples for the most unpredictable reasons—the resemblance to a brother, perhaps, or a shared love of cats, or the enthusiasm in an adoptive parent's voice. This did not reassure us. It all seemed so random. Months would go by with no calls at all. Would the call ever come? Would a birth mother ever choose us over all those other couples? Was this continued failure God's way of telling us He didn't want us to become parents?

We finally were chosen, but even that did not end our anxiety. We met with the pregnant birth mother and got to know her, but the mixed signals she gave kept us uneasy. At one moment she would declare how happy she was that we would raise the child, but in the next moment she told of pressure she felt from family members not to go through with the adoption. She would tell us she would call on a certain day, but then she would not only fail to call but would be out of touch for a few weeks, ignoring our messages. Was she displaying the normal jitters that accompany such a momentous decision, as the lawyer tried to reassure us, or was she toying with us?

She would break her long silences by calling and insisting that everything was on track, that she was absolutely determined to go through with the adoption, and that she wished we would stop worrying. Were family members still pressuring her to change her mind? Would the birth father sign the papers?

We waited and prayed. We announced the impending adoption. We gratefully received gifts at baby showers. We bought a crib, a rocking chair, baby bottles, clothes, formula. We decorated the baby's room. We picked out names.

The birth mother scheduled her Caesarian section. We arranged for time off work. We made plans for out-of-town family to arrive to celebrate with us. The birth mother invited us to go with her to the hospital a few weeks ahead of the birth to make all the arrangements. The lawyer prepared the legal documents.

The Agony of Powerlessness in the Face of Silence

Then, on the day of the birth, silence. The birth mother had disappeared. It was not that she had changed her mind and had informed us or the attorney that she wanted to back out of the adoption. That would have been devastating enough. What made it even worse was that we did not know what she was doing. She had not told anyone her plans, and we had no way to reach her.

How should we interpret her silence? Our attorney once again tried to reassure us that she was probably simply working through her feelings and would contact us when she was ready. She had gone silent before, said the lawyer, and this was no doubt another one of those episodes that would end with her calling up and laughing at us for being worried. These reassurances rang hollow. We tried everything we knew to reach her. We left messages at her apartment. We tried to reach her family members. We called the hospital, which had no information on her. We tried other hospitals in the area to no avail. After a couple days of this silence, our lawyer finally got worried too and made calls of her own. The mystery remained.

I learned some things about silence in the weeks that followed. Whether it is the silence of God in a time of spiritual dryness or the silence of a person in our adoption crisis, *one of the most exasperating aspects of silence is our powerlessness in the face of it*. In many ways, even bad news is better than silence. You can't negotiate with silence. You can't fight it. You can't seek explanations from it. All you can do is cry out against it.

With our adoption, the birth mother's silence brought not only emotional pain but also practical problems. Everyone we knew waited for news of the baby's birth. When should we make the phone calls to tell them the adoption had collapsed? Or had it? The birth mother's life had been marred by time in prison and by abusive relationships. Was it possible that some kind of foul play had prevented her from calling us?

The silence even made it hard to know what emotions to give way to. Should we wait a week before we gave up and let ourselves begin to grieve this disaster? Two weeks? Had the baby been born? Was he all right? Was the birth mother all right? Was she a victim, or were we justified to be angry at her? Had she deceived us all along, or had she merely changed her mind? Should we be angry at the lawyer? Should we be angry at God?

My wife and I were angry, and we were grieving, and we

were worried, and we were hopeful, and we were humiliated, and we were frustrated. We had both taken time off work, expecting that by then we would be changing diapers and doing late-night feedings. We were encased in a silent house, waiting for the phone to ring. The house should have been buzzing with friends and family and the cries of a baby, but instead the stillness of the place was a mockery of our hopes and dreams. We couldn't even stand to look at the baby's room. We shut that door and stayed away from it.

In our prayers, we cried out for God to rescue our situation or at least to make sense of it. Why was this happening? Did He not want us to be parents? Had we been wrong to pursue this dream for so many years? The adoption was not our only problem during those confusing days. I had been diagnosed with melanoma, a deadly form of skin cancer, on my leg and would soon have surgery to remove it. If the cancer had spread, my future would be even more uncertain than it was already. I contemplated the possibility that God had caused the adoption to fall through because I would not live long enough to be a parent. That must have occurred to my wife as well, but neither of us said it out loud. One more bit of silence that was distressing me during those weeks was that I was waiting for an answer from a publisher that was seriously considering a book that I had spent years writing. The publisher's silence had stretched on for six months, and despite my inquiries, they still couldn't give me an answer.

For years now, we had felt stuck in this same place. Doors would never quite open for us, but they wouldn't slam shut either, which would at least have allowed us to give up and knock on a different one. We had reached the end of our resources, not only financially, but also emotionally and spiritually as we wandered around that empty house feeling foolish and abandoned.

How Zechariah and Elizabeth Endured Decades of Silence from God

Perhaps in part because of the struggle that my wife and I went through in our desire to have children, one of my favorite stories from the Bible is that of Zechariah and Elizabeth, who became, to their great surprise, the parents of John the Baptist. It is a profound story of faith and of working through the pain of God's silence until His purpose is fulfilled.

On the day that his amazing biblical story began, Zechariah had the honor of performing his priestly duties at the Temple. He was "getting on in years" (Luke 1:7, NIV), and he had been waiting on the Lord for most of his life in two significant ways. First, like other Jews, he was waiting on God to send the Messiah, a wait that had stretched out over centuries. Second, on a more personal level, he and his wife, Elizabeth—also a devout person—had waited in pain and humiliation for God to bless them with children. In their culture, barrenness was considered a sign of God's disfavor, a punishment for sin.[2] Elizabeth speaks of "the disgrace I have endured among my people" (v. 25) because of her barrenness. And yet, the Bible flatly declares that "both of them were righteous before God, living blamelessly according to all the commandments and regulations of the Lord" (v. 6, NIV).

How inexplicable, how miserable it must have been for Zechariah and Elizabeth to know that they were living true to God's commandments and yet met only silence from Him when it came to the deepest longing of their hearts. They not only had to come to terms with their own disappointment and pain but also had to endure the false assumptions of their community about where they stood with God.

But then one day everything changed. As Zechariah carried out his priestly duties in the Temple, an angel appeared to him next to the altar of incense as the congregation waited outside. "Your prayer has been heard," said the angel (v. 13, NIV). *What* prayer, Zechariah must have wondered, because the childbearing years for his wife and him were long past. Was he still even praying that prayer? The angel continued, "Your wife Elizabeth will bear you a son, and you will name him John. You will have joy and gladness, and many will rejoice at his birth, for he will be great in the sight of the Lord" (vv. 14-15, NIV). The angel went on to tell how John would be filled with the Holy Spirit and would guide people to God.

Zechariah had two responses to this good news. The first, a reaction to the angel's sudden appearance, was *fear:* "When Zechariah saw him, he was terrified; and fear overwhelmed him" (v. 12, NIV). The second response was *disbelief:* "Zechariah said to the angel, 'How will I know that this is so? For I am an old man, and my wife is getting on in years'" (v. 18, NIV). Eugene Peterson's translation of this verse is even more blunt: "Zechariah said to the angel, 'Do you expect me to believe this? I'm an old man and my wife is an old woman'" (TM).

Ironically, considering all the decades of silence from God that Zechariah has endured from God, the punishment that the angel Gabriel gave to Zechariah for his (understandable) skepticism is that Zechariah himself would be unable to speak until the birth of his son occurred. Now *he* would be the silent one. When he went back out to the congregation that had started to wonder what was taking him so long, he had nothing but hand motions to try to explain the astounding encounter.

Elizabeth conceived and gave birth to John, and after Zechariah wrote on a tablet, "His name is John" (v. 63, NIV), he once again was able to speak.

What might Zechariah's story reveal about God's use of silence?

God Was Silent in Zechariah and Elizabeth's Life, but He Was Also Powerfully at Work!

Like Job, who also suffered and who also endured God's silence, Zechariah and Elizabeth were righteous people. Also like Job, even though outsiders wanted to try to attribute the couple's suffering to sin, that was not the reason for it. The fact is that God was fulfilling His purpose in Zechariah and Elizabeth all along! His timing was certainly strange, since we don't normally think of old people having children (with certain notable biblical exceptions, such as Abraham and Sarah). But one of the things that bothers the angel most about Zechariah's doubt is that he seems unable to accept God's bizarre timing. The angel says, "But now, because you did not believe my words, *which will be fulfilled in their time . . .*" (v. 20, NIV, emphasis added). Peterson's translation puts it this way: "Every word I've spoken to you will come true on time—*God's* time" (TM).

Sometimes All You Can Do During God's Silence Is Hold Steady Until Your Sense of His Presence Returns

When the angel appeared to Zechariah after all those long years of unanswered prayer, what was Zechariah doing? Was he sitting alone in a room somewhere, brooding bitterly over the unfair circumstances that God had put him in? Was he acting out his frustration by accusing his barren wife of some hidden sin? Was he seeking revenge on his neighbors who had made false assumptions about him and brought humiliation on him and his wife?

No. He was in the Temple, *carrying out his duties*. Some of the biggest questions of his life were unanswered. He had reasons to be discouraged. Maybe he was. We are not told how he felt. We know only what he did, and that was "living blamelessly according to all the commandments and regulations of the Lord" (v. 6, NIV) and was serving as priest before God and his section was on duty (v. 8).

God rewarded Zechariah and Elizabeth's loyalty and steadfastness. What would God have done if this old couple had given in to the circumstances around them and had turned cynical and disobedient in their old age? How easy it would have been for them to have forfeited their place in His amazing plan for the salvation of the world if they had allowed themselves to give up on God. They did not *hide* their feelings. Elizabeth is blunt about the disgrace she had endured. But regardless of circumstances, they obeyed God.

If there is ever a time to be led by what we *know* instead of what we feel, it is during those times when God's presence seems distant. We have seen over and over that He is unpredictable, full of surprises. If you read the Bible, you will see countless examples of people who endured significant times of God's silence in their lives, from Moses to Joseph to Abraham to Job to Zechariah and Elizabeth. If they would have let the *circumstances* of God's silent years in their lives determine whether or not they would follow Him, they all would have turned away from Him. They all had valid reasons to give up on Him from a purely circumstantial point of view. Instead, they dug in during those years. They held on to their faith because of a *deep-down assurance* in their lives—an assurance that contradicted the evidence of temporary events—that God was *real* and that His ultimate plan for them was *good* and that His promises were *true*.

As a Christian, the times of God's silence in your life are when you may be able to do nothing more than simply take your stand and wait. You will feel like your faith is hanging by a thread—hang onto that thread! You will feel the temptation to walk away from God, if for no other reason than to do something bold and to act in the midst of the void. Resist that temptation! Remember the days when God's presence flooded your life so joyfully. *Know* that His presence will return again. Know that He is working out His plan in you, as strange as the timing and methods may be. Pray for resolve. He will honor that prayer. He will pull you through.

God's Silence Jolts Us Out of Complacency, Keeps Us Dependent on Him

In my own story of our struggle to have children, I see now, as I did not see then, that we had to get to the end of our own plans and schemes and agendas before God broke His silence. All of our efforts to reach our dream of starting a family failed. Not only did those plans fail, but they also brought us physical pain, emotional pain, humiliation, embarrassment, frustration, and large financial costs every step of the way. More specifically, we had complications from infertility medicines, pain from surgery, frustration from the long waits to have our own child and the long waits to adopt a child, embarrassment and humiliation from the adoption processes and failures, and big financial costs from all those steps. A cancer scare and career uncertainty added to our troubles. Like Zechariah and Elizabeth, we had dreams that were not inherently wrong, and a plan to get there that was not unreasonable. However, God had a better way. Would we wait on Him to accomplish it?

I kept a journal during those difficult days, and most of it is filled with bewilderment and anger at the circumstances that engulfed me. But there are a few glimmers of hope too. One entry in the midst of otherwise bad news says, "The words that keep going through my mind are, *God will redeem this situation.*" Another entry says, "*Blessing will flow from this* is the message I keep sensing out of this tragedy with our adoption. I can't tell anyone that because it doesn't make any sense, but I do believe it is a promise of God. He has not abandoned us." Though God was mostly silent, His quiet voice was seeping through.

Once it became clear that the adoption would not happen (the birth mother resurfaced in a few weeks with new promises of putting up her baby for adoption, but this quickly fell through), my wife and I took a trip out of town and took no action at all for a while. After several weeks, we contacted a new attorney at a friend's recommendation, and the whole process started again. On the day we met him, he gave us instructions for compiling a new portfolio that would be given to birth mothers who might select us. That night, I felt utterly exhausted and at a loss, not sure that I could drag myself through this whole thing again. Even routine aspects of the process, like creating another of those portfolios with all the happy pictures and upbeat biographical information, felt overwhelming.

By the *next morning*, however, the new attorney had set up

an appointment for us to meet birth parents who were highly motivated to put up their baby for adoption and who had already tentatively chosen us. How was this possible? Before, we had not been matched with anyone for a year and a half. Now it was less than 24 hours from our first appointment with the lawyer, and we hadn't even begun the portfolio yet. After he met with us, he just happened to have an appointment with the birth parents that evening, and he had our old portfolio in his briefcase. When they read it, they were ready to choose us. We went to the appointment that night almost too stunned to know what to say. After all we had been through, this seemed too easy. The baby was due to be born in two or three weeks, so there would be no more long months of agonizing waiting. We quickly made all the arrangements, and in spite of a few nerve-wracking complications with the hospital bureaucracy, nothing fell through. Less than a month later we took Jacob home from the hospital. God had indeed redeemed our pain.

But there were even more surprises in store. When Jacob was four months old, as I sat in our family room feeding him a bottle, my wife came in and made a startling announcement: she was pregnant. As with the sudden reversal of our adoption fortunes, I was skeptical of this good news. The doctors had said pretty conclusively that this would *not* happen, so I told her she *could not* be pregnant. She had just taken a pregnancy test, she said, and it came out positive. She had been aware of the signs for a while but had tried to explain them away. She didn't want to say anything to me until she took this test, but now it was undeniable. I still didn't believe it. I asked her to take another test. She drove to the drugstore and got one.

While she was gone, my main worry was how she would

handle the disappointment when she found out the first test had been wrong. She came home and got the same positive result. My disbelief wavered. Still, I couldn't fully accept the truth until several days later after her trip to the doctor. Like Zechariah, I had set aside the prayer for my wife's pregnancy and had trouble believing the answer when it came. God did not take away my ability to talk, but I was almost speechless anyway.

Beyond those remarkable answers to prayer, which we considered miraculous, God brought our other crises of that moment to a decisive conclusion. I had surgery to remove the melanoma on my leg, and despite the inconvenience of having to limp around for many weeks, the outcome was positive be- cause the cancer had not spread. As for the publisher that had kept me waiting for most of a year, the editors offered me a contract not only for the book I had proposed but for two oth- ers beyond that as well. I had gotten so used to long waits for everything that waiting had come to seem like a permanent condition. When God broke through those waits and an- swered my prayer, it was hard to take it in. My response to these events in my journal was restrained. In some ways I think I kept waiting for the catch. God had been silent for so long. Did He now really mean to bless us?

This is not to say that the hard days were over. My wife nearly lost the baby early on, and she had to be on partial bed rest for about eight months. But four days short of Jacob's first birthday, our daughter Katie was born, lively and healthy. Anyone looking at my life from the outside might see an American middle-class cliché: I have a wife and two chil- dren—a boy and a girl—who live with me in relatively good health in a house in the suburbs of Southern California. It probably looks as if we planned it all this way. As with so many people's lives, from the outside there is no hint of long, agonizing waits for God to act, of bewildering periods of His silence, of discarded or delayed dreams, and of times when it looked as if nothing would turn out right.

God May or May Not Fix Circumstances to Our Liking, but His Presence Will Return

At the time of our daughter's birth, I thought the answer to the prayers was the real point of those events. Even now, when I'm in a tough time when God seems distant, I look back to that time to remind myself that even though there are discouraging times of crisis and confusion, He also gives us miraculous breakthroughs.

But from a distance of several years, I believe it was just as important that he knocked us off stride, woke us up, made us wait on Him so that we finally realized our complete dependence upon Him for every detail of our family life, our work, even our very existence. I am grateful for the blessing of His answer, but I am also grateful now for the silence and the deeper place that it took us. God acted, but not in the way we asked Him to and not in the timing we wanted. His plan looks perfect to me now. He was silent for a time, but He was never absent.

However, I am also aware that God sometimes breaks these periods of silence in our lives without changing the difficult circumstances that often accompany them. I am intrigued by a point that Philip Yancey makes about the end of the story of Job. At the end of Job's tremendous suffering, including the loss of family, home, wealth, and health, God finally breaks His long silence and speaks to Job. He also restores Job's fortunes, giving him "twice as much as he had before" (Job

42:10) in material possessions, and also seven sons and three daughters (v. 13). As Yancey says, some readers, like Elie Wiesel, believe Job lets God off the hook too easily and that the restoration of fortunes does not make up for the suffering Job had endured. Others interpret the story to mean that God will deliver His followers from adversity and restore health and wealth if only they wait on Him and trust Him.

Yancey believes both interpretations are wrong. After God delivers His "Where were you when I laid the foundation of the earth?" speech, Job is surprisingly contrite, given his earlier complaints, and says to God, "Therefore I have uttered what I did not understand, things too wonderful for me, which I did not know" (v. 3). What readers like Wiesel and others overlook is that "Job spoke his contrite words before any of his losses had been restored. He was still sitting in a pile of rubble, naked, covered with sores, and it was in those circumstances that he learned to praise God."[3]

If the restoration of his fortune was not the reason Job was satisfied, then what was the reason? Yancey writes "I have a hunch that God could have said anything—could, in fact, have read from the Yellow Pages—and produced the same stunning effect on Job. What He said was not nearly so important as the mere fact of His appearance. God spectacularly answered Job's biggest question: Is anybody out there? Once Job caught sight of the unseen world, all his urgent questions faded away."[4] God's silence, not adversity, was what Job found unbearable. When God's presence came flooding back into his life, Job was reconciled to Him in spite of circumstances. Even great suffering becomes more bearable when we know God is there, with us in our pain, and working toward our ultimate good.

Questions for Reflection

1. Think of some times your silence has been misinterpreted. Have you ever been accused of pouting or being angry when in fact you were merely deep in thought or tired? Has someone ever taken your silence to mean approval when it really meant skepticism? Has someone ever interpreted your silence as disapproval when it really meant satisfaction or shyness?

Analyze how these examples are similar and different to times of God's silence. If you are too quick to ascribe reasons for God's silence, how likely are you to get it wrong?

2. When God goes silent, the *powerlessness* of that sometimes leads people to react in ways that harm them spiritually, such as sinking into bitterness or rebelling against God or taking matters into their own hands and trying to force a solution apart from God. Can you think of examples when you or someone you know reacted badly to God's silence? Rewrite that scenario for how it could have turned out better. What lessons can you draw from that for future challenges?

3. Review the story of Zechariah and Elizabeth. What can you learn from them about how to respond during extended times of silence from God?

8

WHY DOESN'T GOD JUST *SAY* IT?

I got a phone call yesterday from a friend in another state whose life is bogged down by money problems and family difficulties. His most immediate problem was that his car—which had already gone many years and tens of thousands of miles beyond its prime—had broken down again, and he had no way to get to work the next day. Even if he could get the car to the shop, he had no money to get it repaired. Even if he could get it repaired and get to work, his job was already hanging by a thread because of his company's threat to move his work to Mexico. He needed to find a new job, but he hadn't been able to land an interview, and even if he managed that, he had no car to get there, and even if he had a car, he would need a haircut for the interview, and he couldn't even afford that.

He hated to complain. He knew many other people were far worse off than he was. His difficulties certainly didn't rise to the level of suffering that many people across the world were going through, with lives thrown into chaos by war, hunger, and disease. Considering all the good things in his life—a loving wife and beautiful young daughter, a good home, and many other blessings—he knew he had much to be grateful for. Still, he felt trapped financially and in other ways, as if everywhere he turned, there was no let-up from stress, no breakthrough. He wondered how God was working in all of this, assuming He was working at all.

"I just don't see what grand spiritual purpose is served by all this," said my friend.

He was a Christian, following the Lord as best he knew how. God's presence was in his life, he supposed, but quite honestly, he didn't see all that much evidence of Him working.

The conversation kept running through my mind after we hung up, and I wondered, what would it do to my friend's faith if God suddenly swooped in and solved all those problems, which certainly would be easy for Him to do?

My friend looks out his window this morning and finds a new car in his driveway. There's even a big red bow on the hood. The car is his. Paid for. In an envelope in the glove box, he finds a pile of cash equal to several months' salary to keep him going while he looks for a new job. There's plenty of money left over, too, for a haircut. A vacation. A new wardrobe.

Will his faith soar? Will he never doubt God again?

Or imagine if God worked that way in your church. This Sunday, instead of the usual music and preaching and small-group meetings, instead of the usual subtle and slow workings of the Holy Spirit in a church that loves God but also faces many problems, God decides to bombard your church with miracles. The first thing that happens is that everyone who walks into the sanctuary that morning receives miraculous physical healing. A woman arrives in a wheelchair but walks out on her own strong legs. A man arrives leaning on a cane but tosses it in the trash can on his way out. A lady hobbles in with horrible back pain, not sure she can bear to sit through the entire service, but she leaves pain-free, leaping into the air.

That's not all.

A man burdened with financial worries opens his church bulletin to find it stuffed with enough money to pay his bills.

Another church member opens her bulletin to find the address and phone number of a friend she had lost touch with. The harried parents of young twin boys find a note from church friends offering to babysit the kids while the couple goes out on a date. Throughout the congregation people find personal answers beyond anything they would have dared hope for.

When the pastor gets up to preach, his words strike at the heart of people's needs and questions. A husband scribbles down words—almost as if they were being dictated by the pastor—that he needs to reconcile with his wife. Others in the congregation receive new understanding of spiritual and theological questions that had perplexed them for years.

What effect will these remarkable incidents have on the faith of this church? Will the congregation be so blown away by God's miraculous movement that they will never stray from Him again? What will it do for their attempts to reach out to the community and draw others into their church?

These sound like wonderful fantasies, but already you may be sensing some problems that might arise. In my friend's case, he certainly would be grateful for the new car and the glove box full of money, but what happens when the car gets old and the money runs out? If I were in his shoes, I know I would immediately go back to God for more. Beyond that, if God is willing to give cars and money, then why not a better house too? And how about a dream job thrown in? Or, if my friend is feeling lazy, how about no job at all but plenty of money to cover expenses?

He certainly would be willing to continue to serve a God like that, but what would it do to his relationship to God? Would he love God, or would he instead fall in love with the miracles? Would he become materialistic, spoiled, self-absorbed, feeling no need for faith or spiritual things? The materialistic gifts that had so enticed him could become his spiritual downfall. Instead of gradually becoming more Christlike as he increased his faith and dependence on God, he instead would move in exactly the opposite direction, demanding more and more of God even as he loved Him less.

A similar fate might befall the church. At first, of course, when word got out of the miraculous healings and the money-stuffed church bulletins, people would no doubt shove their way into the sanctuary on the very next Sunday. Attendance would soar. The church's fame would spread. Television news crews would set up their cameras to try to record every miracle. Newspapers, magazines, Web sites, and blogs would buzz with commentary and analysis of this astounding manifestation of God's power.

In one sense, this attention would provide a perfect opportunity to spread the gospel. The reporters and bloggers would be eager for explanations of these events, and the pastor and church members could share with them the message of salvation through Jesus Christ.

But would anyone be listening to that message? Would the crowds that show up be interested in spiritual truth, or would they instead be more focused on a quick fix to their money woes? Would faith increase, or would greed increase?

And what would happen if several Sundays went by *without* such miracles? Imagine the howls of complaint and the disappointment on the first day that the crowds left the church having received nothing more than the gospel message and a time of worshiping God. What would happen to people's faith then? Who would get the brunt of the blame for this change of circumstances? What if the miracles returned, but only *some* received money and only *some* were healed? What kind of relationship would this set up between the haves and have-nots?

It's easy to see that what started out as a miraculous movement of God greater than anyone could have hoped for could quickly turn into a spiritual mess that could throw the church into turmoil. And yet, in our own lives, wouldn't many of us prefer a more visible, more talkative, more obviously assertive God? On one hand, we're certainly grateful for the way He moves in our lives already. We sense His presence, we see evidence of His working through circumstances, we are deeply grateful for the salvation and joy that life in Him brings. Our faith grows day by day. Having seen what He has brought us through already, we learn to trust Him more and more even during periods when we don't understand His timing and methods.

On the other hand, we think, wouldn't it be nice to see God break out of the self-restraint in which He so often seems to keep himself? For instance, instead of revealing His will to me through prayer in which I receive impressions of the direction He wants me to go, how about sending me an angel, bathed in fire, to tell me word for word unmistakably what He wants? Where is the God with the booming voice that I have so often heard in skits and movies? I would like to hear Him like that. I wouldn't need these miracles all the time, just once a year or so, or even just *once*. One unmistakable supernatural event that I could point people to when I tell them about God. Is that too much to ask?

I wouldn't even insist on a *personal* miracle. I'd be satisfied with God breaking forth into the world to, say, wipe out hunger in an entire country or sweep aside a bunch of terrorists or topple a dictatorship. Witnessing something like that would keep me from ever doubting Him again. It would build my faith and make me trust Him from then on no matter what happened.

Or would it?

If God Appeared in a Blaze of Fire and a Booming Voice, Would It Make My Faith Last?

If anyone experienced the kind of dramatic personal communication from God that I have wished for in my own life, it was John the Baptist. Think of it. From the time he was young he must have been told the story of his miraculous birth to Elizabeth and Zechariah, who conceived long after they were too old to have done so and who were visited by an angel sent to make the announcement.

That story, however, was nothing compared to what John would experience himself. Dressed in camel's hair clothing and eating locusts and wild honey in the desert, John not only *proclaims* the coming of Jesus but also gets to see Him and talk to Him. Not only does he get to talk to Jesus, but Jesus insists that John baptize Him. John feels unworthy to do this, but Jesus says, "Let it be so now; for it is proper for us in this way to fulfill all righteousness" (Matt. 3:15, NIV). Can you imagine being the person chosen to perform the most important baptism in history? Would that be enough to keep your faith strong forever?

But there is more. When Jesus comes up from the water, "suddenly the heavens were opened to him and he saw the Spirit of God descending like a dove and alighting on him" (v. 16). Amazing! Not only is Jesus there, but the Holy Spirit is too. Could it get any better? It does. "And a voice from heaven said, 'This is my Son, the Beloved, with whom I am well pleased'" (v. 17). The booming voice of God the Father! Could John or anyone else ask for anything more confirming of his or her faith and calling? The Father, the Son, and the Holy Spirit are right there with him in such powerful, undeniable ways that he could see and hear. Surely he would never struggle with doubt for the rest of his life.

Except that he does. After the baptism of Jesus, circumstances do not treat John kindly. He ends up in prison. Scripture does not record much detail about what went through his mind there, but Matt. 11:2 says, "When John heard in prison what the Messiah was doing, he sent word by his disciples and said to him, 'Are you the one who is to come, or are we to wait for another?'"

What? After what he has seen and heard, after an encounter with God that goes beyond what almost anyone in history has experienced, does he really need to ask that? How could he not already know that Jesus was the one? In the days of the visible signs of God's presence, with Jesus right there with Him and God's voice calling out from the heavens and the Holy Spirit descending as a dove, it was easy for John to believe. But when he's shut off in a dreary prison, uncertainty creeps in.

John's story illustrates a principle that we find many other places in Scripture and in the hypothetical examples that began this chapter. It is this: the kinds of dramatic signs and miracles that we often long for and that we believe would confirm for us once and for all that God is present in our lives do not in fact produce long-term faith. Instead, deep faith is *nur-*

115

tured gradually as we listen for His voice, spend time with His Word, immerse ourselves in the community of other believers, and trust God as He works slowly and sometimes inexplicably through the various circumstances of our lives. It is a less dramatic and more frustrating process than most of us would prefer, but there is no shortcut around it.

Another clear example of a group whose faith was sustained by dramatic signs from God is the Israelites that Moses led to the Promised Land. These followers of God don't just experience a once-in-a-lifetime miracle. They saw miracles *every day*. God leads them through the desert with a pillar of cloud during the day and a pillar of fire at night. Wouldn't that keep your faith on track? Bread called manna falls from the sky for them to eat each day. These miracles are in addition to the more spectacular ones they witness, such as the plagues against Pharaoh, the parting of the Red Sea, and the destruction of Pharaoh's army.

Even with all those signs of God's presence, they still have trouble trusting Him. When they run into difficulties, they pour out-loud, melodramatic complaints to their leaders. And when Moses leaves them for a while to go up Mount Sinai to receive the Ten Commandments, they go off the deep end completely. As Moses departs, they see a dramatic sign of the presence of God: "Now the appearance of the glory of the LORD was like a devouring fire on top of the mountain in the sight of the people of Israel" (Exod. 24:17, NIV). Shouldn't that be enough to keep them waiting patiently and staying faithful to God until Moses returns? But as the days roll by and there is still no Moses, they get antsy, they worry, they doubt, and finally they give up altogether. Incredibly, after all that God has shown them and done for them, they go to Aaron and urge him to make a golden calf for them to worship. When he does so, they celebrate with a wild, drunken party.

So much for relying on sensational signs and wonders from God to uphold our faith. Could the fact that such overt signs of God's power and presence fail to nourish genuine faith be the reason that He is far more likely to relate to us in a more restrained, sometimes almost hidden and silent manner? Commenting on the portion of Scripture in which Jesus weeps over Jerusalem, Philip Yancey writes, "Jesus, who could destroy Jerusalem with a word, who could call down legions of angels to force subjection, instead looks over the city and weeps. God holds back; He hides himself; He weeps. Why? Because He desires what power can never win. He is a king who wants not subservience, but love. Thus, rather than mowing down Jerusalem, Rome, and every other worldly power, He chose the slow, hard way of Incarnation, love, and death. A conquest from within."[1]

Think back to the story of Zechariah and Elizabeth that we looked at in the previous chapter. It was not the dramatic appearance of the angel or Elizabeth's miraculous birth in old age that sustained their faith. Those things didn't happen until near the end of their story. Their faith was strong because they trusted God and kept living for Him even during the long, silent years when His ways must have seemed inexplicable to them. The same is true of Abraham and Sarah or Joseph in prison or Paul in prison, or dozens of others that could be mentioned. God's restraint does not mean God's absence. He may work quietly in our lives, with timing and methods that we may not always prefer, but He is building faith in us strong enough to stand the test of time.

Sometimes God's Silence and Restraint May Be an Act of Mercy

Nothing is as comforting as God's presence. When His Spirit washes over us during worship or prayer, we're filled with joy. When we witness His hand moving through circumstances, we're encouraged in our faith. When we see evidence of His power in nature, we're filled with awe. When we sense His presence in music, art, and literature, we're inspired.

That's why it's easy to forget how dangerous He is.

We may think we'd be better off if God ripped away His self-restraint and flooded our lives with the full, undiluted power of His presence, but we should actually be grateful that He doesn't do so. As Willard points out, "We may be tempted to cry out, like Isaiah, for God to rend the heavens, come out of hiding and stand before us telling us what to do (Isa. 64:1), but we do not really understand what it is we are asking for when we ask that. Probably it would literally kill us or at least unbalance us if it actually happened."[2]

The danger of God's presence is illustrated in many places in Scripture, such as in Exod. 19, when the Lord prepares to descend on Mount Sinai. The Lord tells Moses, "You shall set limits for the people all around, saying, 'Be careful not to go up the mountain or to touch the edge of it. Any who touch the mountain shall be put to death'" (v. 12, NIV). He later adds, "Go down and warn the people not to break through to the LORD to look; otherwise many of them will perish" (v. 21). Later, when the Israelites worship the golden calf while Moses is on the mountain, God is ready to destroy them but holds back only because of Moses' intercession for them. God sends them on toward the Promised Land, but His anger is so great that He sends an angel to drive out their enemies rather than accompanying them himself. He says, "I will not go up among you, or I would consume you on the way, for you are a stiff-necked people" (33:3). Even Moses is not allowed to look directly into God's face. The Lord tells him, "You cannot see my face; for no one shall see me and live" (v. 20).

Spiritually, God's withholding of His presence is sometimes an act of mercy that gives us time to ask for forgiveness of our sins and turn back to Him. Without His restraint in the immediate punishment of sin, we would all be dead. In Ezek. 20, the Lord tells of the repeated rebellion of the Israelites. Three times in that chapter He tells of the rebellion and follows it with some version of, "Then I thought I would pour out my wrath upon them and spend my anger against them in the wilderness. But I withheld my hand, and acted for the sake of my name, so that it should not be profaned in the sight of the nations, in whose sight I had brought them out" (vv. 21-22).

Although God is sometimes silent in our lives as He withholds punishment and waits for us to turn to Him in repentance in the name of Jesus, it would be a mistake to misinterpret His silence as weakness. Jeremiah warned against this when he said, "They have spoken falsely of the LORD, and have said, 'He will do nothing. No evil will come upon us, and we shall not see sword or famine.' The prophets are nothing but wind, for the word is not in them. Thus shall it be done to them!" (Jer. 5:12-13). His restraint in the face of our rebellion against Him is not weakness, it is love. When we have stepped away from Him into a life of sin, we may try to convince ourselves that His silence means that He doesn't really care what we do. In fact, He cares intently. Our whole lives He is drawing us to Him. He won't force us to turn to Him for forgiveness, but He patiently and quietly waits and calls. As with the

Israelites, His anger will not be restrained forever. The consequences eventually come. But His silence is an interlude in which we may run back to Him and restore our relationship. As 1 John 2:1-2 puts it, "My little children, I am writing these things to you so that you may not sin. But if anyone does sin, we have an advocate with the Father, Jesus Christ the righteous; and he is the atoning sacrifice for our sins, and not for ours only but also for the sins of the whole world."

This chapter has considered reasons why God usually refrains from approaching us in the dramatic, booming-voice, miracle-producing way that we sometimes think we want. The problem is, He also sometimes temporarily withdraws even His more familiar still, small voice from our lives. Why might He do that, and what might those times be doing to us spiritually? We'll consider those questions in the next chapter.

Questions for Reflection

1. Put together your own scenario similar to those that begin this chapter. What encounter with God or what miracle could you imagine that would be so powerful that you would never doubt Him again? After describing that miracle, play out what might happen in the weeks, months, and years afterward. Would that event really sustain your faith?

2. *If you just do this one thing, I'll never ask you for anything else.* Have you ever prayed this prayer? If He does answer it, are you really satisfied forever, or do you find yourself still seeking more from Him?

3. This chapter points out examples from Scripture in which the danger of God's undiluted presence is shown. Can you think of others? (See 1 Sam. 6 for one example.) Do you think there is a tendency in our day to downplay this dangerous aspect of God? If so, why? How do you reconcile a God of love with a God whose unrestrained presence can wipe someone out?

9

GOD IS SILENT: SHOULD I WORRY?

In his book *Why Me? Straight Talk About Suffering*, Lawrence W. Wilson tells of the response of one of his friends to the news that his wife had suffered a miscarriage. The woman called and asked him to tell his wife, "I want you to tell her that God always has a reason, and sometimes nature's way is best." Far from being comforted by this explanation, Wilson resented this explanation of God's action that he heard repeated by a number of other people in the days that followed. Three years later, his wife gave birth to a baby girl who had a rare genetic disorder that caused severe birth defects. The baby required constant care, including special feedings, oxygen, medications, and other treatments. Wilson wrote, "Oddly, many of the same people who had been convinced that God in His mercy had allowed our first child to die were now sure there was some noble purpose in Laurinda being born with a critical illness. The rationale was exactly the opposite of before."

What is Wilson's own explanation for why God allowed him and his family to suffer? He said, "It has been 15 years since Laurinda flickered to life and died. No reason that anyone offered for the death of a child made sense to me then. None makes sense to me now. I don't say that God had no reason for allowing suffering in her life or in mine—I simply have no idea what it might be. And anyone who tells me that he or she does know is a fool. For only a fool would claim to know what God has refused to say."[1]

As we consider what may happen to us during times of God's silence in our lives, we should begin by humbly acknowledging that often we simply don't know why we do not sense God's presence during those periods. In the chapter "Misinterpreting God's Silence," I spoke of the danger involved even in trying to understand *each other's* silences, let alone God's. During our failed adoption described in that chapter, for instance, my wife and I had many possible interpretations for why the birth mother we were working with had lapsed into silence and disappeared. Was she hurt? Was she in jail? Had she changed her mind? Was she about to call us at any moment? Not *all* of our theories about her disappearance could have been correct. *One* might have been right, or they *all* could have been wrong.

Although we will not always know why God's presence seems distant from us at a particular time, that is not to say that we can never know anything about how He uses silence in our lives. Most of the major figures in the Bible endured a period of God's silence in their lives. What can we learn from them? Christians throughout the centuries and fellow believers in our own day have also experienced these painful and bewildering periods when God seems distant. How did those times change them? What might God's silence mean?

Sometimes God Is Silent Because We Are Not Listening to What He Already Told Us

Jesus' disciples were often confused by what He said. His parables often baffled them, and they had to ask Him to explain them. When He used words like *bread* or other terms metaphorically, such as comparing His body to the Temple, they often missed the point. However, they also sometimes misunderstood Him even when He spoke as plainly as it was possible to speak. In Luke 9:44, for example, Jesus tells them, "Let these words sink into your ears: The Son of Man is going to be betrayed into human hands" (NIV). Pretty straightforward, isn't it? No allegorical language to interpret. No hidden spiritual message. *I am about to be betrayed.*

They didn't understand. Eugene Peterson's translation of the following verse captures their bewilderment well: "They didn't get what he was saying. It was like he was speaking a foreign language and they couldn't make heads or tails of it. But they were embarrassed to ask him what he meant" (v. 45, TM). Why couldn't they understand these simple words? Perhaps because it wasn't what they wanted to hear. It was not what they were prepared to hear. The words didn't fit the story they thought they were living.

How do the disciples handle their confusion? Do they ponder Jesus' words until they finally make sense of them? Do they go to Him and ask for clarification? No. instead, they change the subject—drastically. The very next verse says, "They started arguing over which of them would be most famous" (v. 46, TM). What? Jesus has just spoken to them about an upcoming event that not only will transform His life and theirs forever but will also alter the course of human history. They brush that aside without a word and move immediately to a topic closer to their hearts—which of them will win the rivalry to outdo the others. After they talk about that issue, they move on to other concerns. The subject that Jesus raised never gets brought up again for many chapters. When He finally *is* betrayed, they are surprised. Jesus was not silent about what was going to happen to Him, but they were paying attention to other things.

How often are we just like them? We want to talk about one thing, but God wants to talk about another. For example, perhaps you want God to reveal how He is going to lead you in your calling or what future spouse He has in mind for you or how He's going to help you get out of the financial mess you're in. You pray, you read Scripture, you listen for His leading, but He is silent on those subjects. Instead, the scriptures that stand out to you and the impressions that you receive from God as you listen during prayer deal with other things entirely—your problems with anger or the shoddy way you've been treating people around you or the way that greed has made you more and more materialistic and self-absorbed. You complain, Why won't God answer my prayers? Why is He silent on the things that matter most to me? In fact, He is not silent at all, but you have cut off His voice on issues that you find uncomfortable and have tried to change the subject.

Maybe it's time for you to step back and review what God may have been revealing to you recently in Scripture, in sermons, in books, through friends, through prayer, and through circumstances. Are you listening, really listening, to Him?

Most parents know the exasperation of repeating a message to their children over and over but knowing that it is not getting through. After the consequences strike, and the glass that was sitting too close to the edge of the table really does get knocked off and breaks or someone really does get hurt playing that way or they really do feel wiped out the next morning after staying up too late, it is not uncommon for them to say something like, "Why didn't you tell me?" They often want to point the finger of blame at someone else, as if the warnings had not been clear. The parents' frustration is only a tiny hint of the profound sadness and disappointment

God must have felt over the centuries as His followers repeatedly ignored the messages He sent so clearly.

One of many places in the Bible where this is illustrated is in 2 Kings 15—17, which gives a litany of one king after another who failed because they refused to heed God's clear commands. "In God's eyes he lived an evil life" is the conclusion recorded about one after another of them, for generations. God's anger with the people's refusal to listen to Him culminates in chapter 17, which says, "They had accumulated a long list of evil actions and GOD was fed up, fed up with their persistent worship of gods carved out of deadwood or shaped out of clay, even though GOD had plainly said, 'Don't do this—ever!" (vv. 11-12, TM). The following verses point out that God had spoken "clearly through countless holy prophets and seers time and time again," but the people "wouldn't listen. If anything, they were even more bullheaded than their stubborn ancestors, if that's possible" (vv. 13-14, TM).

God may be silent about some matters in our lives that we wish He would address, but are we listening to the vast amount of truth He has already revealed through the Bible and in other ways? It may be pointless for us to seek a new word from the Lord if we are ignoring His clear word that is already right in front of us.

God's Silence on Specific Issues May Mean We're Free to Decide for Ourselves

Should I take that job? Should I marry that person? Should I sell my house and move to another state?

When we face big decisions like those, as Christians we naturally turn to the Lord for guidance. Often we sense His calling in a certain direction and can take action—or cease from taking action—confident that we are acting within His will. We know from experience that He guides us not only in the big decisions of life but often also in seemingly smaller matters. Many Christians have felt the Lord impressing them to call a friend who may need a sympathetic ear or to give money to a certain ministry in their church or to strike up a conversation with a particular stranger in a waiting room or airport lobby.

But this desire to seek God's will can become twisted or even paralyzing if we begin to expect that the Lord is going to give us specific guidance on every decision we have to make. He doesn't. He remains silent on many of the particulars of our lives, but we may go forward confidently, knowing that as we abide in Him, we have great freedom to make a variety of choices that fall within God's will. As Willard says, "There is also, after all, a neurotic, faithless, and irresponsible seeking of God's will: a kind of spiritual hypochondria, which is always taking its own temperature, which is far more concerned with being righteous than with loving God and others and doing and enjoying what is good."[2]

If we expect a word from the Lord about every little decision, we trivialize what it means to be His follower. What color upholstery should I choose for my car? What outfit should I wear today? Which newspaper article should I read first? Certainly there are rare times when such seemingly insignificant details might matter for some reason unknown to us, and God can certainly break in with a word on them, but the normal course of things is that He won't, and we are free to decide for ourselves. Just as parents teach their children to make their own decisions on an increasingly wide range of issues as the kids get older, so God gives His children a wide realm of freedom to make their own choices, any of which would please Him.

Willard offers a helpful approach for a Christian in a well-functioning relationship with God to seek His will on particular matters. The first step is to bring the matter to the Lord, and then listen for His guidance. James Dobson describes his own process for doing this: "I get down on my knees and say, 'Lord, I need to know what you want me to do, and I am listening. Please speak to me through my friends, books, magazines I pick up and read, and through circumstances.'"[3] The next step is to go on about your business of the day, listening for an impression from the Lord if it comes. Willard writes down these impressions for further study, sometimes discussing them with friends. If no impression comes, then he keeps a general attitude of listening but in a reasonable amount of time goes on to make his own decision. He believes that God does not play games with us, and God will give us guidance on the things that truly matter: "Direction will always be made available to the mature disciple if without it serious harm would befall people concerned in the matter of the cause of Christ."[4]

God's Silence May Be a Natural Pause as He Works Out His Long-Term Plans

I wish God would give me daily reassurances of where He is taking me. I would love to have His constant encouraging message, *You're on the right track. You're doing fine. Keep moving in this direction. You made the right decision back there. Here is where you're headed next, and here is how you're going to get there.* It doesn't usually happen that way. Sometimes God breaks into my life with reassuring signs of

His presence and direction, but often there are long intervals without anything.

A recent experience in a nonspiritual realm of my life helped shed some light on why God may not rush to reassure me as much as I would like. My wife and I hired a contractor to put in a new driveway and block wall at our house. He and his crew ripped out the old driveway, which left behind a field of dirt and debris. No problem. We knew the new driveway would soon fill that space. But then the contractor backed up his truck onto that space to unload the blocks he would use to build the little wall at the driveway's edge. He backed up a little too far and smashed his truck into the corner of the house, right next to the garage door. Now we had a debris field for a driveway, a smashed-in corner of the house, a garage door that no longer functioned, and piles of stone blocks scattered all about.

The contractor apologized profusely for his accident and promised to fix everything to look as good as new. Then he went silent. When the next day rolled around and neither he nor any of his crew showed up, we got worried. When another day after that came and went without any word from him, we began to imagine all kinds of possibilities. Had he taken off, never to be seen or heard from again? Did he figure that fixing his error would be so expensive that it was better to abandon the project altogether and hope that he could get away with it? Would this turn into a legal battle? Would our driveway remain a dirt hole and would our garage wall be caved in for weeks or months to come? We left messages for him. We waited. Another silent day went by.

Then he reappeared. He was smiling, upbeat, ready to get back to work. He told us of the arrangements he had made to fix the garage wall and then to complete the rest of the project. Why had he been silent? Not because he was planning to abandon us. Not because he did not plan to live up to his commitment. He had been purchasing the materials and arranging the workers to get the job done. That afternoon they started, and in due course we had a repaired garage wall and a new driveway. The contractor was not as communicative as I would have preferred him to be each step of the way. But from his perspective, during those silent days there was no reason for him to contact us. His job was to put everything in place to finish the project, and he assumed we would trust him in the meantime.

In the way He communicates, God is not all that different from our contractor. As He is working in our lives, He may not give us as many details and updates and time schedules as we would like. Once He points us down a path, He may require us to walk a long way in silent faith before we hear from Him again.

We should not feel singled out. This is the way He dealt with many of the most important figures in the Bible. Look at Abraham, for example. Few people are more important in the biblical narrative, and few people have more recorded conversations with God. However, these conversations are separated by *many years* of silence, and even when God speaks, He does not supply many crucial details about His plan for Abraham. In Gen. 12, God tells Abram to go to the land of Canaan: "I will make of you a great nation, and I will bless you, and make your name great, so that you will be a blessing" (v. 2, NIV). Once Abram gets to Canaan, the Lord says, "To your offspring I will give this land" (v. 7). The problem is, Abram is already 75 years old, and his wife is barren. The Lord does not deal with those details.

In later conversations, God repeats His promises to Abram, with inspiring words such as, "Look toward heaven and count the stars, if you are able to count them. . . . So shall your descendants be" (15:5). Years slip by. Abraham keeps waiting, keeps listening, keeps believing, but God keeps *not explaining* how He intends to make His plan come true. I try to put myself in Abraham's place and wonder how I could possibly have handled God's silence and kept believing in the face of circumstances that made the fulfillment of God's plan look so unlikely. Abram's wife Sarai continues to be childless, and she urges Abram to have a child through her slave-girl Hagar. Ishmael is born when Abram is 86.

By the time Abram is 99 and Sarai is 90, the opportunity for them physically to have children seems long past, and God has not filled in many gaps in their understanding of His methods or timing. But that's when He reappears to make their dreams come true. God says, "As for me, this is my covenant with you: You shall be the ancestor of a multitude of nations. . . . I will make you exceedingly fruitful; and I will make nations of you, and kings shall come from you" (17:4, 6).

How will this happen? Sarah will have a child. Ninety-year-old Sarah? She laughs at the thought, but it happens. Could there be anything stranger than this way of doing things? Decades of silence, punctuated by God's amazing promises, fulfilled by His methods that no one could have imagined or predicted. Yet as Christians, don't you find Him working that way with you? He's more silent than you'd like. His promises are so bold you're sometimes afraid to believe, yet if you do hold on in faith and trust, He brings you through, more often than not in ways that you never could have dreamed.

132

Yancey describes God's long silences this way: "A flash of light from a beacon on shore and then a long, dreadful time of silence and darkness—that is the pattern I find not only in the Book of Job, but throughout the Bible."[5] This may not be how I would prefer God to work, but just *knowing* that His silences are not unusual helps make them more bearable. I know that during those times, I need to simply keep following the path He has set before me. His timing may not always make sense to me—I might want Him to go faster. His seemingly roundabout methods may not fit the course of action I would have chosen—I would blast away obstacles and head more directly for the goal. His ways are different from my ways, so I learn to hang on in faith. I learn to trust Him. He may be silent more often than I prefer, but I know that He will not speak one word less than I need to hear.

Questions for Reflection

1. This chapter begins with a story of people offering hurtful speculation about the reasons for a family's suffering. Lawrence W. Wilson responds, "Only a fool would claim to know what God has refused to say." How could Wilson's friends have responded to him and his wife in a more helpful way?

2. "We want to talk about one thing, but God wants to talk about another." Can you think of a period in your life when your pleas to God about one subject were answered with impressions from the Holy Spirit, messages from Scripture, and so forth, about an entirely different topic? Were you able to listen to what God was telling you? How did you work through that, and how did it change your perspective on the issue that concerned you?

3. This chapter suggests that God is sometimes silent on particular issues because He has given us the freedom to decide for ourselves. Think back to a major decision you had to make in which you sensed a clear impression from God. Now describe a decision in which you sought God's will but ultimately sensed Him pushing you in no particular direction. What were the indications you went by in both cases? Were there ways that you tested your decision? How helpful do you find the ideas of Dallas Willard and James Dobson mentioned in this chapter?

4. Review the story of Abraham summarized in this chapter. If you were Abraham, how do you think you would have been tempted to respond during those long years of God's silence? Would it have been hard to keep believing God's amazing promises? What implications does this have for your own spiritual journey today?

10

WHERE GOD'S SILENCE MAY TAKE US

I recently watched a father take his five-year-old son to the boy's first basketball lesson. The noncompetitive program was set up to teach the kids the fundamentals of dribbling, shooting, throwing the ball to teammates, and other basketball skills. Of the dozen or so boys and girls on the court that day, this little boy was the least skilled. When he tried to dribble, the ball sailed away from him, and when another child bounced the ball to him, he had trouble grasping it.

He had enthusiasm, though, and the coach was happy to work with him. The father was eager for his son to succeed, too, and unfortunately, that became the problem. The man hovered at the edge of the court, commenting on the boy's every move, issuing a steady stream of advice. Trying to process such a barrage of messages, the boy got flustered and bobbled the ball even more than before.

Then things got even worse. The coach led the kids through a series of drills, and whenever he gave the boy a command—"shoot the ball" or "pass the ball"—the boy's father repeated it word for word, as if the child was capable of understanding a phrase only if it came from *his dad's* mouth. The boy didn't know which man to listen to. The coach's words came from one direction, but before the boy could do what he said, the father would jump in to speak from the other side of the court, and the boy would flub his move because he would glance over at his dad.

The best outcome would have been for someone to have

told the father, "Be quiet. Go sit down. Your boy won't learn if you keep interfering."

Nobody, not even the coach, said anything to the father. He was so intent on giving advice that he probably wouldn't have listened anyway.

When it comes to our Heavenly Father, He knows better than this earthly father when to keep quiet. As Christians, we may think that we would be better off if God was *never* quiet. The more we sense the joy and comfort of His presence, the better. We want Him directing our steps as clearly as possible. We want His attention, His encouragement, His affirmation more and more. As we grow and mature in our faith, we may think that He would be less silent as we come to know Him better. We may expect that the emotional aspect of our walk with God would only increase as our faith itself increases.

In fact, faith does not always work that way. St. John of the Cross, in his classic work *Dark Night of the Soul*, compares the maturing Christian to the infant who gradually needs less constant attention as she matures:

> Once the soul has completely surrendered to serving God, she is nurtured and caressed by him, just like a tender baby with its loving mother. The mother holds the child close in her arms, warming it with the heat of her breasts, nourishing it with sweet milk and softened foods. But as the baby grows, the mother gradually caresses it less. She begins to hide her tender love. She sets the child down on its own two feet. This is to help the baby let go of its childish ways and experience more significant things.[1]

God gives spiritual infants lots of attention. Think of the overwhelming emotions that are part of the Christian life for many of us when we first become believers. The Holy Spirit floods our lives with joy, gratitude, and zeal. We take pleasure in every aspect of this new Christian journey. Worship songs bring us to tears as God's Spirit flows through the music. We drink in messages from the pulpit, the small groups, the long conversations with other Christians. The words we read from the Bible seem to be targeted directly at us. We are hungry for more and more spiritual food. We have a hard time understanding why not everyone around us feels gripped by this same enthusiasm toward the things of God.

As a teenager, I was particularly emotion-oriented in my faith. If God had withdrawn the strong sense of His presence in my life in any way, if He had been like the mother who puts the toddler down to let her start walking out there on her own, I'm not sure my faith could have endured it. But just as overwhelming joy came easily to me, doubt came easily too, and faced with a period of God's silence, I might have given up.

Now, many years later, I have learned that God operates across a much wider emotional range than I could have imagined back then. During periods of His silence, though they are distressing, I have learned to hold on and let Him do His work in this spiritual desert until the joy of His presence floods over me again.

For many of us, the Christian life is full of people and spiritual practices we love. We live our lives in a community of Christians in churches that encourage us and help us grow in our faith. When we face tragedies, these fellow believers are there to help us through. When good things happen, they are there to celebrate with us. We worship, serve others, see new believers brought into the church, see children raised up to become believers. We study Scripture, pray, and sing.

These are all good aspects of Christian life, but there is a danger in them, which is that our connection to the spiritual practices and habits may become stronger than our connection to God himself. These spiritual benefits begin not to *point* us to God but to *replace* Him. Do I enjoy my church so much because it is pushing me forward spiritually or because it is soothing and familiar? Am I more in love with being a Christian than I am in love with Christ? Have I become so lost in the pleasures of the Christian life that I have begun to serve an image of God that is static and tame?

As Christians, how easy it is to rely not on God himself but on our own self-congratulatory concept of ourselves as Christians. In other words, we are believers, so we begin to complacently believe that we have God on a string and that as we follow Him, He will answer our prayers in a predictable way and see to it that we enjoy the fulfillment and comfort that are due us. We skim along on the spiritual surface, avoiding pain and maximizing the "juicy spiritual feelings." We just want to raise our families, do our jobs, enjoy ourselves, and not be bothered.

But then, if we are really following Christ, there are times when He yanks that flimsy scaffolding away from us. He is silent until He has our attention. We had been so pleased with our spirituality and its reassuring rewards, but now the nourishing spiritual stream of God's presence that had flowed into us has dried up. We cry out to Him like a baby whose bottle has been yanked away after only a few sips. As St. John of the Cross puts it, when Christians such as this "are going about their spiritual practices with the greatest enthusiasm and pleasure and it seems to them that the sun of divine favor is shining most brightly upon them, God suddenly darkens all that light. He slams the door shut. He cuts off the source of the spiritual waters they had been drinking from in God as often and as deeply as they desired."[2]

During Times of Spiritual Drought, How Do We Respond?

When we are thrown into one of these times of spiritual dryness, what should we do? A better question to start with might be, what should we *not* do? One inclination may be to blame ourselves for our own lack of zeal or emotion. In order to regain it, we might try to force God's voice back into our lives by frantic spiritual activity. We pray more fervently and insistently. We fast. We throw ourselves into the ministries of the church. We intensify our Bible reading. Still we are dry. What now? We have no other tools at our disposal.

At the opposite extreme, we may sink into discouragement during these times. We may be plagued by doubt—*maybe I'm not a real Christian. Maybe Christianity itself isn't true. Maybe I should give up on God.* Our frustration may turn outward toward other people. We may resort to blame—*it's my church's fault that I've grown spiritually dry. This pastor isn't as good as the last one. This new music stinks. The people in the church aren't as dedicated as they used to be. How can I expect to flourish spiritually in such an atmosphere of compromise and hypocrisy?*

Blaming others gets us nowhere, of course, so we are back where we started. The irony is that when we are experiencing God's silence, we usually see it as a sign that we are being led away from God's love. In fact, it may actually be a sign that we are moving into His blessing as He prepares us to move to a deeper spiritual level. Our inclination is to fight these times of silence, but perhaps instead we should welcome entering into this time—though painful—when we have absolutely nothing but God to rely on. Mirabai Starr, a recent translator of *Dark Night of the Soul*, describes the prayer that the believer prays in the dark night: "Plunge me into the darkness where I cannot rely on any of my old tricks for maintaining my separation. Let me give up on trying to convince myself that my own spiritual deeds are bound to be pleasing to you. Take all my juicy spiritual feelings, Beloved, and dry them up, and then please light them on fire. Take my lofty spiritual concepts and plunge them into darkness, and then burn them. Let me only love you, Beloved. Let me quietly and with unutterable simplicity just love you."[3]

If we pray this prayer, then what else is there for us to do? Wait on God. Hang on to our faith. Let God do His work in us in the silence. We will be like Job, who held on to his faith during God's silence. It won't be easy. It will probably take much longer than we think it should. We will get antsy. We will be tempted to take control of the process instead of quietly trusting God. Shortly after the Israelites were freed from Pharaoh in Egypt after hundreds of years of slavery, they found themselves stuck in the desert. God was guiding them, but Pharaoh thought, "They are wandering aimlessly in the land; the wilderness has closed in on them" (Exod. 14:3, NIV). Still angry about having lost his slave labor force, he sent his army out to bring them back. Knowing that Pharaoh's soldiers were about to swoop down on them, the Israelites panicked, and they turned their fear on Moses, sarcastically complaining, "Was it because there were no graves in Egypt that you have taken us away to die in the wilderness? What have you done to us, bringing us out of Egypt?" (v. 11).

Moses' response contained wisdom that can help us through our own fearful times in the spiritual desert, when we feel abandoned by God. He said, "Do not be afraid, stand firm, and see the deliverance that the LORD will accomplish for you today; for the Egyptians whom you see today you shall never see again. The LORD will fight for you, and you have only to keep still" (vv. 13-14, NIV). *Stand firm. The Lord will fight for you. You have only to keep still.* These may be the only tools available to us during the most severe times of spiritual dryness. We have to *wait* on God and let Him do His work in us in the silence. Like Job, we *hang on* to our faith despite our inability to make sense of God's seeming abandonment of us. Simply waiting on God, however, goes against our inclination. St. John of the Cross writes:

> The soul might continue to have qualms about wasting time. She may wonder if it would not be better to be doing something else, since she cannot think or activate anything in prayer. Let her bear these doubts calmly. There is no other way to prayer now than to surrender to this sweet ease and breadth of spirit. If the soul tries to engage her interior faculties to accomplish something, she will squander the goodness God is instilling in her through the peace in which she is simply resting.

> It would be as if a painter were composing a portrait and the model kept shifting because she felt she had to be doing something! She would be disturbing the master's work, preventing him from accomplishing his masterpiece.[4]

In the case of the Israelites, when they waited on God to accomplish His purposes His own way, He did so in ways they never could have anticipated. Who could have predicted He would part the Red Sea and drown Pharaoh's army in it? Nothing they could have done on their own could have brought that about. As Pharaoh's army rushed toward them, the evidence they saw might have indicated that God had abandoned them to that despot, but nothing could have been further from the truth. God had a plan to rescue them all along, *though He kept silent about what that plan was*. The Lord fought the battle for them. Their task was to stand firm. Keep still. Don't give in to fear. If we do that in our own desert times, eventually our sense of God's presence—with the joy, the reassurance, the comforting sense of being deeply loved—will come flooding back. We will emerge changed, having gone deeper spiritually in ways that nothing else could have accomplished.

Our Greatest Spiritual Victories May Come When We Are Least Aware of Them

Cut your age in half for a moment, and think about what your life was like at that earlier age. If you're 30, go back to age 15. If you're 60, go back to 30.

As you look back to those days, think of the various ways in which the details of your life have changed between then and now. How much of that change was completely unpredictable?

As I write this, I am 45 years old. At 22, I could not have predicted where I now live, where I work, who I am married to, when my children were born, where I go to church, who my closest friends would be, what technological gadgets now fill my days, and hundreds of other details. All these changes came about so gradually that I don't often stop to consider how vastly different my life is now compared to then.

Looking back, I can now see God's hand in situations in which He seemed absent at the time. That is not to say that *all* the disruptions and calamities of the past 20 years now make sense, of course. Some of those times still look like pointless tragedies and dead ends. Maybe in eternity I'll see how God was working even in those circumstances, but already the passing of years reveals that God has often been moving in surprising ways even during periods that felt devoid of His presence.

During my freshman year of college, for instance, I felt adrift when, a month or two into the school year, I realized I no longer wanted to study to be a journalist as I had planned to do all through high school, and I didn't want to stay at the college I was at. The year seemed wasted. I had gone into college so confident that I was following my passion and God's plan for my life, and then it all turned sour. I couldn't even transfer until the next year, so I spent the rest of that school year feeling as if I were wasting time. I worried that even when I switched majors and schools, the same pattern might repeat itself—an early enthusiasm followed by dread that I had taken the wrong path. I prayed, but I felt little reassurance or direction from the Lord. He was quiet, as if even He didn't want to get stuck with me in this dead end and had turned His attention elsewhere.

Now, many years later, I see that period much differently. That one year of journalism helped me get part-time jobs throughout college and graduate school. I'm actually glad now that I had to stay there for an entire year to keep taking journalism courses and writing newspaper articles. That experience benefits me to this day, as I write books and teach college writing courses. I no longer see that period as a time when God abandoned me to some pointless blind alley. Instead, I sense His careful leading through a difficult but useful year.

I can think of many other times of God's silence that I have had to reinterpret. After graduate school, I got my dream job, which soon turned into a big disappointment. I turned to God to make sense of this, but His answer was silence. Eventually, however, that discontent led me to an even better position in another state, where I met my wife and where I've had the most productive years of my career. In an earlier chapter I described our years of infertility and failed attempts at adoption, during which we called out to a silent God. Those setbacks gave way to the adoption of our son and the birth of our daughter, outcomes even better than what we dared to pray for in the days when God seemed to ignore us.

As human beings tied to a particular time and place, our perspective is understandably narrow. It's easy for us to think that the routine life we see before us is all there is. We do our best just to get through each day, not expecting much to happen. But what if we knew that the Lord was drawing us into an ongoing story much bigger than ourselves, an epic battle of good and evil raging behind that partition that veils the spiritual realm? We sometimes see evidence that we are in a spiritual battle, but at other times it is going on—and we are soldiers in it—even though we see and hear nothing.

Some of the biblical figures whose stories we have already looked at, such as Zechariah and Elizabeth, are good examples of this. As parents of John the Baptist, these two were significant soldiers in the spiritual war of the ages. However, until the angel appeared to Zechariah when he was an old man carrying out his duties in the Temple, they knew nothing but

God's frustrating silence. God knew all along that He would call on them at the proper time to play their part, but He didn't tell them. However, to his and Elizabeth's credit, they were willing to step into their assignments. Like good soldiers who had to stand guard for months on a deserted battlefield until the war came to them, Zechariah and Elizabeth had remained faithful to God during their years of disappointment. They had no idea what God was preparing behind the scenes.

What about us? What might God be preparing for our lives? If the veil were pushed aside and we could peek behind the scenes, how might that help us to make sense of the bewildering periods of aridity and stalled dreams? We are rarely if ever allowed to see behind that partition in this life, but if we stay ready as Zechariah and Elizabeth did, I believe God will redeem those long, dry spells eventually and lead us to our unique role in the great spiritual war of the ages. I keep a paper on my desk that says, "The most amazing things may happen," and I believe it. I can hardly wait to see what God will do next.

The story of Job is another example in which God's silence on the surface masks dramatic divine activity and attention behind the scenes. The story begins with a wager between Satan and God: will Job remain faithful to God even when all of God's blessings are stripped away from him? Job loses family members, possessions, and his health, but even in his horrible suffering, what bothers him most is that God stays hidden and silent. He complains, "Why do you hide your face, and count me as your enemy?" (Job 13:24). That is how it appeared to Job, but was God really absent? No! He was paying close attention. So was Satan. Job was at the center of the showdown between them. Job, however, had no way of knowing this.

From his perspective, he was all alone, crying out to a silent God who no longer cared about him. Yancey comments, "From Job, we can learn that much more is going on out there than we may suspect. Job felt the weight of God's absence; but a look behind the curtains reveals that in one sense God had never been more present."[5]

Ironically, it is when Job is at the lowest point in his life—suffering misery and loss and feeling abandoned by God—that he is achieving his greatest spiritual victory and that his actions are most significant to God and, as readers of his story, to us. During his earlier years enjoying the abundant blessings of God, he may have believed that God was more attentive, but it is actually during his *struggle* that God has given Job a more important role to play in a momentous battle of good versus evil. "Yes, there was an arm wrestling match," writes Yancey, "but not between Job and God. Rather, Satan and God were the chief combatants, although—most significantly—God had designated the man Job as His stand-in. The first and last chapters make clear that Job was unknowingly performing in a cosmic showdown before spectators in an unseen world."[6]

God likes to surprise us.

Think of all those times in Scripture when God or His angels show up in people's lives and blow away all their expectations. He may do the same to us. Sometimes He uses dramatic circumstances to shake us out of our old ways of thinking and open us to His better plan. But just as often, He uses silence to do that. He uses it to push us into the place where only Jesus can rescue us. In reality we were always already in that place, but often we fool ourselves into believing we can get by on luck or cleverness or contacts or some other personal resource. In silence, those props get pulled out from under us. We are left with some choices—we can turn to God and put our complete trust in Him, regardless of what we don't see or don't hear at this moment; we can frantically increase our own vain efforts to make God conform to our own designs; or we can sink into a quiet despair in the belief that life is mostly a series of random hopes and disappointments.

Getting to the end of our own resources so that we at last are open to His more amazing way is often painful. St. John of the Cross said:

> Many find themselves wishing that God would only be aligned with their desires! It makes them sad to have to want what God wants. They have an aversion to adapting their will to God's. They may even have convinced themselves that if something does not please them and correspond with their will, then it must not be God's will, either, and that if they are satisfied, then God must be too. They measure God by themselves and not themselves by God. This is not in harmony with the teachings of the Gospel which say: "He who loses his will for God shall gain it and he who desires to gain it shall lose it."[7]

When Elijah takes his journey into the wilderness in 1 Kings 19, he asks the Lord to let him die. He lies down under the broom tree and falls asleep. The angel comes to give him food and drink and then sends him on a 40-day trip to Horeb, the mount of God. When the Lord finally speaks to him after those weeks in the wilderness, Elijah has no request or plan to present to God. Ruth Haley Barton comments, "It is interesting that Elijah never asked for guidance; guidance simply came in the context of his willingness to be with God in utter openness and vulnerability. Something in the willingness to stop the flow of his own words and listen in silence opened up the space for the one who longs to speak and offer guidance for our next steps and knottiest questions."[8]

In our own days in the wilderness we can rest assured that God is present, and when the time is right, as we wait and listen, He will speak into our lives again if we hold steady and let the silence do its work.

Questions for Reflection

1. One of the statements in this chapter is, "As Christians, how easy it is to rely not on God himself but on our own self-congratulatory concept of ourselves as Christians." What does that mean? Do you agree that this is a problem? If so, what are some specific ways it happens?

2. In Exod. 14:13-14, Moses tells the Israelites, "Do not be afraid, stand firm, and see the deliverance that the LORD will accomplish for you today; for the Egyptians whom you see today you shall never see again. The LORD will fight for you, and you have only to keep still." Can you think of a time in your life when you felt led by God to simply stand firm, keep still, and let the Lord fight your battle for you? Are there other times when you had to do just the opposite, fighting with all your might? How can you tell the difference?

3. During your journey as a Christian, how have your emotions toward your faith fluctuated and changed? What range of emotional orientations have you seen among the Christians you admire? How reliable is emotion as a gauge of the depth of a person's spirituality?

4. This chapter points out that "God likes to surprise us. Think of all those times in Scripture when God or His angels show up in people's lives and blow away all their expectations." Make a list of all the people in the Bible whose lives were radically changed by God's unexpected intervention. In what ways has God surprised you in your own life? Were all those surprises welcome? As Christians, how flexible does God require us to be with our plans and expectations? How hard is that for you?

A Guide for Personal or Group Study

SILENT GOD
Finding Him When You Can't Hear His Voice

by
Joseph Bentz

INTRODUCTION TO THE STUDY GUIDE

What Is *Silent God* About?

As Christians, many of us confront periods in our lives when God goes silent. For reasons that are unclear to us, we don't sense His loving, powerful presence as we once did. Although we are not in open rebellion against God, and although we've been following Him as best we know how, He seems more distant than ever, and our spiritual lives are dry. What is wrong? *Silent God: Finding Him When You Can't Hear His Voice* offers a fresh approach toward the pain and bewilderment—as well as the mystery and power—of intervals of God's silence in the Christian journey.

One of the reasons we may lose our sense of God's presence is the noise of our lives drowns Him out. We are bombarded by the physical noise from freeway traffic and televisions and other people's music and hundreds of other noises that assault us from morning to night, but even worse is the mental clutter that floods our brains in the form of e-mail, cell phones, media voices, Web sites, and many other sources. In one sense, we may love all this commotion. It makes us feel vibrant, connected. We may even become *addicted* to this buzz, constantly checking e-mail and cell phone messages and filling nearly every moment with *some* kind of sound. We do the same with our schedules, cramming in more and more, wearing our busyness as a badge of success and importance. As the noise in our lives accumulates, we don't deliberately block out God, but we simply find ourselves living in such a state of spiritual clamor that we lose the desire or ability to settle down and really commune with Him and listen to Him.

We are not powerless, however, to quiet the noise and reconnect with God. *Silent God* explores practical and valuable ways of getting the noise of our lives under control and reaching a state of spiritual sanity.

Noise, however, does not explain every period of God's silence. This book also considers ways He uses silence to work out His spiritual purposes in our lives. The Christian life is full of comforting spiritual benefits and practices, but the danger is that our connection to the spiritual practices and habits may become stronger than our connection to God himself. These spiritual comforts begin not to *point* us to God but to *replace* Him. When we are truly following Christ, there are times when He yanks that flimsy scaffolding away from us. He is silent until He has our attention. We reach the place where we have nothing to rely on but Him alone. We face dangers during these painful periods, such as misinterpreting God's silence, turning to cynicism, or giving up on Him altogether. But when we hang on during these times, allowing Him to do His work, God's presence comes flooding back, and we emerge not only more spiritually mature but also amazed at the surprising ways in which He carries out His design in us.

How This Guide May Help You

Silent God is well-suited for use in small groups, Sunday School, and for personal study. I have had the pleasure of teaching portions of the book to two different classes while I was writing it. I have written this guide to help you in your personal study or to lead a small group through these issues of God's silence. The book itself contains questions at the end of each chapter for discussion or reflection, and this guide provides additional suggestions for activities, questions, and examples that are not included in the book.

1

CRYING OUT TO A SILENT, SLEEPING, HARD-OF-HEARING GOD?

Key Questions and Activities

Is God's voice growing fainter in our world?

That question may be a good one to start your study of this book. What are the first impressions when asked that question? How would it be answered at this early point in the study?

Because the purpose of this chapter is simply to introduce the main issues the book will address, you may want to combine the study of this chapter with the next chapter if you are working in a group. The first chapter will help you establish the *relevance* of the issues of God's silence in people's lives. Here are some questions that may help you set the stage for what is to follow:

When God Goes Silent

1. Read the scripture verses that begin this chapter. Did they surprise you? When the writer addresses God with complaints such as, *"Get up, GOD! Are you going to sleep all day?"* or *"GOD, don't shut me out; don't give me the silent treatment, O God,"* does that strike you as being too disrespectful toward God? What kind of relationship do you suspect the writer had with God in order to feel comfortable enough to be this blunt with Him? Do you ever speak that way to Him yourself?

2. Can you think of a specific time when you felt the depth of frustration with God's silence that is illustrated in the opening scriptures and in the excerpts from other psalms quoted near the end of this chapter? Think about that time. Did other people know you were in such a desperate state, or did you keep it to yourself? How did you handle it? What are other ways people

sometimes handle such periods? Rebellion against God? With-
drawing from Him and from other Christians? Sinking into cynicism? The rest of this book will offer perspectives on ways to
emerge from those times having grown deeper in your faith.

Bombarded by Noise!

1. Review the first few pages of this chapter. How is *noise* defined
   in those pages? Make a list of the various ways that "noise"
   manifests itself in our lives.

2. After looking at your list, what spiritual impact do you think
   such noise may have on you? This book will examine the impact of noise in our lives as Christians and will show ways of
   quieting the noise that drowns out God's voice.

Where This Study Is Headed

From what you have read so far in this opening chapter, what
stands out to you as the idea or question you most hope to explore in your study?

Key Quote

"For some, disappointment or tragedy ushers in a period when
God seems far off. His silence can descend on us during times of
doubt and during times when we are running from Him. At other
times we cannot point to any known cause of such a painful period. We have been following the Lord for years, but the closeness
of His Spirit fades, and we feel spiritually stuck, adrift. The worship
services, the music, the prayer that used to embody His presence
now leave us cold. A cynicism may develop in us—toward the
church, toward fellow believers, toward God himself. Where we

once were full participants in the Body of Christ, we now stand aloof and set ourselves up as critics of all things Christian. We get good at pointing out all the flaws in the church and in other believers."

Key Scripture

"GOD, don't shut me out; don't give me the silent treatment, O God" (Ps. 83:1, TM).

2

SILENCE FROM GOD—WHY SHOULD WE EXPECT ANYTHING ELSE?

Key Questions and Activities

Most Christians believe that being a believer means having a personal relationship with Christ. We believe God speaks to us. However, most of us are also skeptical about some of the messages that people sometimes attribute to God.

I'm going to give a list of several statements that have been attributed to God. Read these statements and rate them on their degree of believability on a scale of 1 to 10, with 10 being the most believable. Ask yourself or your group why the statement is believable. This will lead to fascinating thoughts about *how* God speaks to us and how we sense His presence in our lives. It also reveals various ways that people sometimes try to *manipulate* God's voice to serve their own purposes.

Statements to Rate

1. "God told me that He wants you to put an extra $500 in the offering next week."

2. "I felt God's presence in the worship service today."

3. "If you want to know God's will for your life, all you need to do is read the Bible."

4. "When I got fired, I took it as a sign that God was telling me to change careers."

5. "God told me that if I turned left in the parking lot and went down the third aisle, I would find a parking spot."

6. "Being a Christian means having a personal relationship with Christ."

Union with Christ

The scriptures quoted in this chapter describe a startlingly close and loving relationship that Christians can have with God. While much of *Silent God* deals with times of God's silence, those times should be the exceptions, not the rule, in the lives of Christians. This chapter refers to Dallas Willard's concept of the movement of our relationship with God from *communication* to *communion* to *union*. When Paul talks of Christians "having the mind of Christ," for example, that is certainly union, but what does it mean?

One way to understand what union with Christ means is to compare it to the marriage relationship. If you are married, or if you are doing the study with a group that includes married couples, this exercise is a good way of exploring the idea of "having the mind of" someone. Married couples can serve as examples for this activity.

Jot down, or ask couples to jot down, answers to the following questions:

1. You go to your favorite restaurant. What will your spouse order?

2. Your spouse is annoyed with you. How can you tell?

3. Your spouse does not want to be bothered. How do you know?

4. You're not with your spouse, but an invitation comes up that you know he or she would like. How can you tell?

5. You have bad news to deliver to your spouse. How accurately can you predict his or her reaction?

Do any of these answers illustrate "union"? Do any of the answers illustrate "having the mind of" someone? How is that different from reading someone's mind? How is it different from communion or communication?

This can lead to a discussion of the meaning of "union" with Christ. How is it similar to and different from the examples from marriage? Analyze the scriptures given in this chapter. Describe what that union is like in the life of a Christian who is living it. What activities, attitudes, habits, and character traits will be evident in such a person?

Key Quote

"Scripture is filled with God speaking—extravagantly and in a startling variety of ways—into people's lives. He spoke to Moses from a burning bush, He spoke to Jesus, Elijah, Moses, Peter, James, and John from a "light-radiant cloud" on the Mount of Transfiguration, He spoke from the midst of a blinding light to Paul on his way to Damascus. I could give dozens more examples, but the point is this: *we can be confident that God is reaching out to us.*"

Key Scripture

"Abide in me as I abide in you. Just as the branch cannot bear fruit by itself unless it abides in the vine, neither can you unless you abide in me" (John 15:4).

3

IS GOD TOO QUIET, OR IS THE WORLD TOO NOISY?

Key Questions and Activities

Our lives are noisier than we realize. This chapter points out that most of us are not fully aware of how much energy we spend each day blocking out noise from crowds and cars and televisions and neighbors and countless other sources. What impact does all this noise have on us in the long run? Do we get so good at blocking out sounds that we also inadvertently filter out God's voice?

Just How Noisy Is It?

• Make a list of noises that most annoy you. Will this list include things like people talking in movie theaters? Neighbors who have loud parties while you're trying to sleep? What else? Once the list is complete, ask:

• What is it precisely that makes these noises so bothersome? What do they prevent you from being able to do? Sleep? Concentrate? Sustain a creative train of thought? Relax? Pray? Listen?

• Think through a typical day and note all the sounds that you must block out in order to function. Are you surprised by how long this list is?

• Sit in silence for five minutes. Afterward, ask, was it really silent? What sounds did you hear that you otherwise might not have been aware of? Was sitting in silence uncomfortable? Was it hard to settle into it? Did you feel restless enough to want to break out of it and make some sound of your own?

So It's Noisy—Who Cares?

• Review the story of the Newport Beach residents who were turned into "sleepless zombies" by the constant barking of the packs of sea lions near their homes. One of the residents said that she gets little sympathy from outsiders when she complains how bad the noise is. How sympathetic are you to her plight?

Is a person's right to quiet—or a person's desire for quiet—something people in our culture take seriously? Or is other people's noise something we're simply supposed to be willing to put up with? How well is your own desire for quiet respected in the neighborhood where you live? In your workplace? In your own home?

• What is there about noise that we *like*? Do we associate it with excitement, fun? Do we use it to block out unpleasant thoughts?

• What spiritual impact might addiction to noise have on us? Do you know people who want some kind of sound around them almost every minute? Do those people find it difficult to sit alone in a room and spend time in deep prayer, meditation, and listening to God? Can the noises of life block out God's voice even though it's not our intention to let that happen?

What Next?

You may choose to close your session by letting your group know that just as this chapter dealt with physical noise, the next one will deal with psychological noise. After that, the book considers strategies for reducing all types of noise in your life.

Key Quote

"We're not really supposed to mind the concentration-breaking, sleep-stealing noise. Isn't it simply a part of life that we can't do anything about? Some people live with it so long that they no longer even *want* to get rid of it. People who are used to having the television on all the time for background noise get very uncomfortable when it is turned off. People who are used to a blaring TV volume are frustrated when it's turned down to a more conversational level, even though they can easily hear it."

Key Scripture

"Be still, and know that I am God!" (Ps. 46:10).

4

DROWNING IN AN
ELECTRONIC FLOOD

Key Questions and Activities

Cell phones, e-mail, video games, Web pages, radio shows,
TV news reports, newspapers, magazines, billboards, commercials.
These are only some of the sources of the psychological noise that
assault us every day. In one sense we love these noisy gadgets.
We spend lots of money to bring these things into our lives and
spend lots of time paying attention to them.

However, we may also become addicted to them, overwhelmed by them, and practically enslaved to them. They may eat
away at the time we spend with other people. They may drown
out any moments of solitude we would otherwise enjoy. And perhaps most dangerously, they may lure us away from a desire to
spend time alone with God.

This chapter will allow you to examine the psychological noise
level in your life and think about how you can prevent the valuable
technological tools of our day from becoming your masters.

A Typical Noisy Day

This chapter begins with the scenario of a man unable to settle
into his work for the afternoon because of the distractions of
phone calls, e-mails, and the Internet. Describe a similar scene in
your life. List all the distractions that prevent you from concentrat-
ing throughout the day. Is the list longer than you thought it would
be? Has the problem gotten better or worse in recent years?

Debate: Are the Gadgets Good or Bad?

In a discussion of psychological noise and the technology that
causes it, it's easy for the conversation to veer to one extreme or
the other—either people say cell phones and video games are

curses on humanity or else they vigorously defend their own gadgets against any suggestion that their devotion to them could get out of control.

One good way to achieve a balanced approach is to list reasonable arguments for the view that the technological tools of our era are marvelous creations that make life better. Then list arguments for the view that the gadgets are time-consuming, concentration-sapping, relationship-destroying, solitude-stealing blights on modern life.

After looking at both arguments fairly, do you feel you can learn to enjoy the benefits of new technology without becoming slaves to them?

If you want to think about this even further, here are some specific items you may want to consider:

Addicted to Psychological Noise

Think about what this chapter says about the *addictive* quality of our technology, from e-mails to television to BlackBerrys to video games. Do you agree that they're addictive? If so, what ones are you most tempted by? How does the addiction work in your own life or in the lives of people you know? How can one break free from it?

Isolated by Technology

Consider the studies and examples cited in this chapter about the ways in which cell phones, computers, and other devices isolate us from one another. Do you agree that interpersonal relationships have changed as a result of these new technologies? What differences have you noticed in the last 10 years? The last 5 years?

The Spiritual Impact of Multitasking

Consider this quote from the chapter:

"The real problem is that a noisy interior life *lures* us away from Him. In the clatter that fills our brain, our faith becomes merely one more item that we try to multitask. Jesus said, 'Abide in me as

I abide in you. Just as the branch cannot bear fruit by itself unless it abides in the vine, neither can you unless you abide in me' (John 15:4, NIV). If a noisy mind makes it hard to concentrate on work or even to sleep, then how much harder will that noise make it to achieve union with God? And when our thoughts are so fragmented and frazzled, will we even lose the *desire* to draw so close to Him? Will we continue to pay homage to Him, but only at about the same level of commitment that we devote to our favorite TV show or Web site? Abiding is the opposite of Instant Messaging. Will He be speaking—or waiting to speak—but we don't even hear Him?"

Do you agree that a noisy brain can lead to such spiritual danger?

Key Quote

"Many of us spend much of our days this way, with our thoughts chopped into little pieces as we jump from e-mail to phone call to quick conversation back to e-mail and then off to some Web sites. All the while our frustration builds because those things in our lives that require blocks of time or unhurried focus— such as meaningful work, a satisfying conversation with a friend, deep prayer, attentive study of God's Word—get postponed, rushed through, or set aside altogether."

Key Scripture

"For you did not receive a spirit of slavery to fall back into fear, but you have received a spirit of adoption. When we cry, 'Abba! Father!' it is that very Spirit bearing witness with our spirit that we are children of God" (Rom. 8:15-16, NIV).

5

REDUCING THE NOISE, CLUTTER, AND AGITATION THAT BLOCK GOD'S VOICE

Key Questions and Activities

After two chapters that established the pervasiveness of the physical and psychological noise in our lives, this chapter and the next one move into specific steps Christians can take to reduce that noise and create more possibilities for solitude, balance, and a closer relationship to God.

Contrasting States of Mind

Think about your noisy self and your quiet self:

What do you see as the most important characteristics of each one, using examples from the book as well as details from your life?

• How helpful are Carl Honore's concepts of slow thinking and fast thinking" and Edward Hallowell's C-State and F-State in understanding these selves?

• How difficult is it for you to balance the two selves in your life? In which direction are you most likely to go out of balance?

Ten Ways to Keep the Quiet Self Alive

This chapter proposes 10 activities and habits for leading you "into that quieter, more receptive, more perceptive state in which you are truly able to listen to God and abide in His presence."

• Don't check e-mail or other messages until as late in the day as possible.

• Get more sleep.

• Cut out one television show or one hour of Internet time a day and spend that time in silence, meditative prayer, or Bible reading.

- Walk or jog—quietly.
- Review all your activities and commitments. If you find that your life is too noisy, decide on one activity that you can set aside in order to simplify your life.
- Take time to enjoy the moment. Draw attention to life's simple pleasures.
- Set aside time to think.
- Do one thing a day to unclutter the space in which you live and work.
- When driving alone, make your car a sanctuary of solitude and prayer.
- Serve others.

Think about each of these activities and then prioritize them from 1 to 10, from most helpful to least helpful.

Are there any of these you would leave out?

Are there any you would add?

Which of these would you challenge yourself to put into practice in the coming week?

Key Quote

"Many Christians allow their entire spiritual lives to drift into this automatic mode. They go through the motions of attending church as habit dictates, praying according to tradition, reading the Bible or ignoring it as time permits, praying halfheartedly as the feeling strikes. It's not that these Christians *intend* to lead shallow spiritual lives, but it feels like that's all that circumstances allow. What can be done to break through to a deeper level?"

Key Scripture

"But now more than ever the word about Jesus spread abroad; many crowds would gather to hear him and to be cured of their diseases. But he would withdraw to deserted places and pray" (Luke 5:15-16).

6

FINDING GOD IN THE SILENCE

Key Questions and Activities

Busy people may believe that the joys of solitude and times alone with God are luxuries they simply can't afford. The previous chapter looked at simple ways to build in some solitude even into a hectic schedule, but sometimes we reach a place of spiritual burnout or crisis in which those steps are not enough.

This chapter examines possibilities for taking a personal spiritual retreat, whether that be for an afternoon, for a week, or even longer. It also looks at ways of making a daily time of listening to God in silence a more meaningful part of the Christian life. Your first impression of a spiritual retreat may be, "I could never do it. I don't have time. I wouldn't know where to begin." There are many ways of finding time alone with God.

Planning the Ideal Retreat

Using the ideas from this chapter and from any other sources that may be helpful, brainstorm plans for a personal spiritual retreat. Among the issues you may want to consider are:

• What *place* might you choose in your area for a retreat? How many possibilities can you think of?

• *How long* would you make the retreat? Would the length of time vary depending on whether or not this is your first time to do this?

• What *activities*, such as prayer, singing, journaling, hiking, reading, would your retreat include?

• If reading is part of your retreat, what books would you bring?

• What *schedule*—if any—would you plan for your retreat?

Think about the benefits and drawbacks of various approaches.

The Obstacles to Taking Retreats

You may still resist the idea of a spiritual retreat because of practical concerns.

Difficulties you may face will probably include things such as taking time off work, family responsibilities, expense, fear of loneliness, and others.

Look at that list and see if you can come up with creative and realistic ways of overcoming those obstacles in order to make a retreat possible. For example, if a weekend retreat is too expensive or time-consuming, how about an afternoon or evening alone? What if you took an afternoon retreat one week and your spouse took one the following week?

Spiritual Retreats: Learning from Others

Robert Benson, Jane Rubietta, Ruth Haley Barton, Henri J. M. Nouwen, Kenneth Leech, and Mark A. Moore are some of the authors mentioned in this chapter who have excellent ideas for how to make the most of spiritual retreats.

What ideas do these writers offer about prayer? Silence? Overcoming the practical difficulties of finding times of solitude? Other issues?

Learning from Jesus' Approach to Solitude

If anyone had a good excuse for being too busy to find times of solitude with the Father, it was Jesus. The demands on Him during His public ministry were unending, yet throughout the Gospels He is shown slipping away to pray. Review the section in this chapter on Jesus' approach to solitude, and ask yourself what lessons you can learn from Jesus' approach to silence and prayer.

Key Quote

"Solitude and silence are not only for a chosen few. They are not only for those who abandon jobs and responsibilities to spend time alone with God. The methods vary widely, but anyone can practice them. The hard part is making the commitment to move forward. *The key is not to let your hesitation over finding exactly the right method keep you from beginning.* This chapter will look at ways that people have managed to do it."

Key Scripture

"In the morning, while it was still very dark, he got up and went out to a deserted place, and there he prayed" (Mark 1:35, NIV).

MISINTERPRETING GOD'S SILENCE

Key Questions and Activities

What does someone's silence *mean*? What does God's silence mean?

These are questions we often ask, and whether we are dealing with other people or with God, it is easy to get it wrong if we make too many assumptions. This chapter examines how to avoid misinterpreting God's silence in our lives during those periods when we cannot sense His presence.

He Loves Me, He Loves Me Not

• Review the story that opens this chapter of the book. Do you sympathize with Amy, who agonizes over the possible reasons why her phone doesn't ring even though Brandon has promised to call her? How might you have reacted in her situation?

• Can you think of examples when your own silence has been misinterpreted by friends, family, coworkers, and others?

Zechariah and Elizabeth: Holding Steady in the Midst of God's Painful Silence

Read the Zechariah and Elizabeth story from Luke 1 and review the commentary on it from this chapter of the book. Then—

• Write an alternate outcome to the story of Zechariah and Elizabeth. In this version, they interpret God's silence toward their desire to have children to mean that He doesn't care about them. Instead of standing firm in their faith and trusting Him, they turn against Him. How would the story have turned out?

• In what ways can Zechariah and Elizabeth serve as role models to us when we face times of silence from God?

• When God goes silent, the *powerlessness* of that sometimes leads people to react in ways that harm them spiritually, such as sinking into bitterness or rebelling against God or taking matters into their own hands and trying to force a solution apart from God. Can you think of examples when you or someone you know reacted badly to God's silence? Rewrite that scenario for how it could have turned out better. What lessons can you draw from that for future challenges?

Key Quote

"As Christians, even when we are practicing the kinds of spiritual disciplines like solitude and prayer discussed in the previous chapters, most of us will experience times in our lives when God goes silent. For reasons unknown to us, we feel the pain of the withdrawal of His presence. Our spiritual lives go cold. Not understanding what is happening, we may panic. We may rebel. We may sink into discouragement. Tragically, we may misinterpret God's silence and give up on Him altogether.

That doesn't have to happen. As strange as it may sound, God may be doing some of His most significant spiritual work in us during those dry times. How can we cling to our faith and let the silence do its work? How can we avoid the trap of misconstruing God's silence?"

Key Scripture

"For he has said, 'I will never leave you or forsake you'" (Heb. 13:5, NIV).

8
WHY DOESN'T GOD JUST *SAY* IT?

Key Questions and Activities

For many Christians, God's approach toward relating to us seems far too restrained. Although it's inspiring to sense His presence in times of worship and prayer and to see His movement in the circumstances of our lives, it would be even better if He would burst into our lives with a steady stream of miracles that would dazzle us and astonish everyone around us.

Or would it?

This chapter examines some possible reasons why God's restraint may be better for us than His overwhelming outpouring of miracles and signs would be. We may think we would prefer the God portrayed in so many movies—with the booming voice and astounding displays of power—but there are reasons that He more often chooses the still, small voice, or at times even silence.

What If You Got Everything You Wanted?

This chapter describes a scenario in which incredible miracles are unleashed on a church. It's thrilling at first, but then it all turns sour. Review that section, and then sketch out a similar miracle scenario for yourself. What miracles would you most like to see happen? Put them all in, no matter how extravagant the list. Then think about what would happen over the course of the following months and years. Would the miracles truly sustain your faith, or would this turn into the same kind of spiritual mess that happens to the church described in this chapter?

If You'll Just Do This One Thing . . .

"God, if you will just do this one thing for me, I'll never ask for anything else."

Think about a time in your life when you have prayed this prayer or something similar. If God did answer that prayer, did it really satisfy you forever, or how long was it before you were back asking for the next "one thing"? How do you account for this aspect of human nature? Does our lack of fulfillment by whatever the "one thing" is serve a spiritual purpose?

"Are you the one who is to come . . . ?"

John the Baptist witnessed God's miraculous power in ways that few people in history have seen or heard, yet he still sent disciples to ask Jesus, "Are you the one who is to come, or are we to wait for another?" (Matt. 11:2). Think about this story. Do you sympathize with John? Do you think you would have reacted similarly as you sat in prison hearing about what Jesus was doing? What implications does this story have for your own journey of faith?

How Dangerous Is God?

Experiencing God's presence is one of the greatest joys of life, but His power can also be deadly. Write down some examples given in this chapter of the danger of God's undiluted presence. Try to think of as many other examples from Scripture as you can.

Then ask yourself:

• Do you think there is a tendency is our day to downplay this dangerous aspect of God? How do you reconcile a God of love with a God whose unrestrained presence can wipe someone out?

• What concepts of God do people carry in their heads? Think of various descriptions and images that people have of Him. In what ways are they true? In what ways are they false?

• What impact might our image of God have on how we interpret the way He uses silence in our lives? Do you think Christians today tend to be more patient or less patient than earlier generations with times of God's silence as He works out His long-term plans in our lives? How might Christians 100 years ago or 200 years ago have seen God differently?

Key Quote

"The kinds of dramatic signs and miracles that we often long for and that we believe would confirm for us once and for all that God is present in our lives do not in fact produce long-term faith. Instead, deep faith is *nurtured* gradually as we listen for His voice, spend time with His Word, immerse ourselves in the community of other believers, and trust God as He works slowly and sometimes inexplicably through the various circumstances of our lives. It is a less dramatic and more frustrating process than most of us would prefer, but there is no shortcut around it."

Key Scripture

"Now the appearance of the glory of the Lord was like a devouring fire on top of the mountain in the sight of the people of Israel" (Exod. 24:17, NIV).

9

GOD IS SILENT: SHOULD I WORRY?

Key Questions and Activities

Although we cannot always know why God is silent on particular issues in our lives or during certain periods, Scripture and experience do show us some of the ways that He uses silence. This chapter examines some of those ways and may help us understand our own struggles when God is silent.

We Ask About One Thing, He Answers About Another

In the chapters leading up to this one, we have looked at how painful and confusing God's silence can be, but are there things you *don't* want to hear from Him about? Are there topics you *avoid* praying about (attitudes, behaviors, fears), and impressions and messages from Him you *resist*?

• Look again at the passage from Luke 9 presented in this chapter, in which Jesus tries to tell His disciples about the coming betrayal He will endure. The disciples brush this aside, not understanding His clear words, and move on to a topic more to their liking—which of them will win the rivalry to outdo the others. After considering this story, think about the following:

• "We want to talk about one thing, but God wants to talk about another." Can you think of a period in your life when your pleas to God about one subject were answered with impressions from the Holy Spirit, messages from Scripture, and so forth, about an entirely different topic? Were you able to listen to what God was telling you? How did you work through that, and how did it change your perspective on the issue that concerned you?

It's Your Decision

This chapter suggests that God is sometimes silent on particu-

lar issues because He has given us the freedom to decide for ourselves.

• Construct a scenario in which you had to clear *every* decision—no matter how tiny—with God. Visualize a typical day of decision-making in which prayer and specific guidance from God had
to accompany every choice, from which breakfast cereal to choose
to which shirt to wear. How long would it take before that method
of determining "God's will" completely broke down?

• Think back to a major decision you had to make in which you
sensed a clear impression from God. Now remember a decision in
which you sought God's will but ultimately sensed Him pushing
you in no particular direction. What were the indications you went
by in both cases? Were there ways that you tested your decision?
How helpful do you find the ideas of Dallas Willard and James
Dobson mentioned in this chapter?

The Rhythm of God's Silence in His Long-Term Plan

Abraham is discussed in this chapter as an example of a biblical figure who endured years of God's silence. Abraham had God's
promises to cling to, but the circumstances of his life gave no indication of when or how God would fulfill them. In fact, if Abraham
went by circumstances alone, he easily might have concluded that
God was not going to fulfill those grandiose plans. Review this
part of the chapter and then ask yourself:

• Who are people you can think of in the Bible who faced a situation similar to Abraham's—God was working their lives but
stayed silent for many years as He worked out His plans?

• How did these biblical figures handle God's silence? Did any
of them *fail* at trusting God during the silent times? How might
history have been different if they had *given up* on God during the
silence? What can we learn from them about how God may work
in our own lives?

Key Quote

"God may be silent about some matters in our lives that we wish He would address, but are we listening to the vast amount of truth He has already revealed through the Bible and in other ways? It may be pointless for us to seek a new word from the Lord if we are ignoring His clear word that is already right in front of us."

Key Scripture

"They didn't get what he was saying. It was like he was speaking a foreign language and they couldn't make heads or tails of it. But they were embarrassed to ask him what he meant" (Luke 9:45, TM).

10

WHERE GOD'S SILENCE MAY TAKE US

Key Questions

It's natural for us as Christians to fight against God's silence and to equate feelings of spiritual dryness with spiritual failure. This chapter challenges those attitudes and shows that times when God feels most distant may in fact be times when He is doing some of His most significant spiritual work in us.

In Love with God or with "Juicy Spiritual Feelings"?

Christian friends, a comfortable church, uplifting music, prayer, Bible study—these are some of the benefits of living the Christian life. As this chapter points out, however, there is a danger that "these spiritual benefits begin not to *point* us to God, but to *replace* Him. Do I enjoy my church so much because it is pushing me forward spiritually or because it is soothing and familiar? Am I more in love with being a Christian than I am in love with Christ? Have I become so lost in the pleasures of the Christian life that I have begun to serve an image of God that is static and tame? As Christians, how easy it is to rely not on God himself but on our own self-congratulatory concept of ourselves as Christians."

When this happens, "there are times when He yanks that flimsy scaffolding away from us. He is silent until He has our attention. We had been so pleased with our spirituality and its reassuring rewards, but now the nourishing spiritual stream of God's presence that had flowed into us has dried up. We cry out to Him like a baby whose bottle has been yanked away after only a few sips."

Ask yourself:

• Do I agree that there is a danger of Christians falling in love with spiritual benefits rather than falling in love with God? Do I agree that Christians sometimes rely on their own self-congratula-tory sense of themselves as Christians rather than on God himself? If so, then how would I recognize that this has happened? What would the signs of it be?

• Have I had any experience with God "ripping away the scaf-folding" of spiritual pleasures and going silent for a time? What are the biggest temptations I must fight during a time like this? What advice would I give other Christians who are facing a time like this?

God Likes to Surprise Us

• This chapter points out that "God likes to surprise us. Think of all those times in Scripture when God or His angels show up in people's lives and blow away all their expectations." Make a list of all the people in the Bible whose lives were radically changed by God's unexpected intervention. In what ways has God surprised you in your own life? Were all those surprises welcome? As Christians, how flexible does God require us to be with our plans and expectations? How hard is that for you?

The Spiritual Act of Standing Still

• Although our spiritual lives sometimes call for courageous action, there are other times when the bravest thing we can do is stand firm and trust God to bring us through our crisis. In Exod. 14:13-14, Moses tells the Israelites, **"Do not be afraid, stand firm,** and see the deliverance the Lord will accomplish for you today; for the Egyptians whom you see today you shall never see again. **The Lord will fight for you,** and **you have only to keep still"** (emphasis added). Can you think of a time in your life when you felt led by God to simply stand firm, keep still, and let the Lord fight your battle for you? How hard is this for you? Is it harder than taking ac-tion? How can you tell the difference between this kind of total dependence on God and simple laziness?

Cut Your Age in Half and Consider What God Has Done

• Review the final section of this chapter, in which the author suggests this activity:

Cut your age in half for a moment, and think about what your life was like at that earlier age. If you're 30, go back to age 15. If you're 60, go back to 30. As you look back to those days, think of the various ways in which the details of your life have changed between then and now. How much of that change was completely unpredictable?

Make a list of the details of your life now that you never could have predicted then. Are there situations you can look back on in which you now see that God's hand was at work even though that was not apparent at the time? How does this change your perspective on how God may be working in your life now? How much of our lives do we have to spend somewhat in the dark about where God is taking us? What might Job or Zechariah and Elizabeth have to say about this?

Key Quote

"What about us? What might God be preparing for our lives? If the veil were pushed aside and we could peek behind the scenes, how might that help us to make sense of the bewildering periods of aridity and stalled dreams? We are rarely if ever allowed to see behind that partition in this life, but if we stay ready as Zechariah and Elizabeth did, I believe God will redeem those long dry spells eventually and lead us to our unique role in the great spiritual war of the ages. I keep a paper on my desk that says, 'The most amazing things may happen,' and I believe it. I can hardly wait to see what God will do next."

Key Scripture

"For I am convinced that neither death, nor life, nor angels, nor rulers, nor things present, nor things to come, nor powers, nor height, nor depth, nor anything else in all creation, will be able to separate us from the love of God in Christ Jesus our Lord" (Rom. 8:38-39, NIV).

NOTES

Chapter 1

1. Terrill Yue Jones, "24/7, Teens Get the Message," *Los Angeles Times*, June 23, 2005, A1, A24.

2. Robert Benson, *Living Prayer* (New York: Jeremy P. Tarcher/Penguin, 1999), 96.

3. Edward M. Hallowell, M.D., *CrazyBusy: Overstretched, Overbooked, and About to Snap! Strategies for Coping in a World Gone ADD* (New York: Ballantine Books, 2006), 9, 10.

Chapter 2

1. Dallas Willard, *Hearing God: Developing a Conversational Relationship with God* (Downers Grove, Ill.: InterVarsity Press, 1999), 56.

2. Ibid., 70.

3. St. John of the Cross, *Dark Night of the Soul* (New York: Riverhead Books, 2002), 28.

4. Rick Warren, *The Purpose-Driven Life: What on Earth Am I Here For?* (Grand Rapids: Zondervan, 2002), 85.

5. Erwin Raphael McManus, *The Barbarian Way* (Nashville: Nelson Books, 2005), 13.

6. Willard, *Hearing God*, 155.

7. Edward W. Desmond, "A Pencil in the Hand of God," *Time*, December 4, 1989, <http://www.time.com/time/magazine/printout/0,8816,959149,00.html>.

Chapter 3

1. Carl Honore, *In Praise of Slowness: How a Worldwide Movement Is Challenging the Cult of Speed* (San Francisco: HarperSanFrancisco, 2004), 121.

2. Ibid.

3. Hallowell, *CrazyBusy*, 56.

4. Roy Rivenburg, "Newport's War on Sea Lions," *Los Angeles Times*, September 15, 2005, A1.

5. Ibid., A25.

6. Corey Kilgannon, "Under the Elevated Track, a New Sensation: Silence," *New York Times,* December 21, 2005, <http://www.nytimes.com/2005/12/21/nyregion/nyregionspecial3/22q>.

7. John Balzar, "A Voice for Silence," *Los Angeles Times,* November 15, 2005, F5.

8. Ibid., F4.

Chapter 4

1. Reuters, "Chicago Hotel Helps Clients Beat Blackberry Addiction," Fox News, June 8, 2006, <http://www.foxnews.com/printer_friendly_story/0,3566,198697,00.html>.

2. Fia Curley, "Detox Clinic Opening for Video Addicts," Associated Press, Breitbart.com, June 8, 2006, <http://www.breitbart.com/news/2006/06/08/D81489R80.html>.

3. Ibid.

4. Hallowell, *CrazyBusy,* 57.

5. Ibid., 58.

6. Claudia Wallis, "Are Kids Too Wired for Their Own Good? The Multitasking Generation," *Time,* March 27, 2006, 49-50.

7. Ibid., 50.

8. Shankar Vedantam, "Social Isolation Growing in U.S., Study Says," *Washington Post,* June 23, 2006, A03, <http://www.washingtonpost.com/wp-dyn/content/article/2006/06/23>.

Chapter 5

1. Hallowell, *CrazyBusy,* 97.

2. Honore, *In Praise of Slowness,* 47.

3. Ibid., 120.

4. Ruth Haley Barton, *Invitation to Solitude and Silence* (Downers Grove, Ill: InterVarsity Press, 2004), 55.

5. Ibid., 56.

6. Honore, *In Praise of Slowness,* 33.

7. Barton, *Invitation to Solitude and Silence,* 60.

8. Joseph Bentz, *When God Takes Too Long: Learning to Thrive During Life's Delays* (Kansas City: Beacon Hill Press of Kansas City, 2005).

9. Anne Fisher, "Be smarter at work, slack off," CNNMoney.com, March 17, 2006, <http://money.cnn.com/2006/03/16/news/economy/annie/fortune_annie0317/index.htm?cnn=yes>.

10. Ibid.

11. Hallowell, *CrazyBusy,* 62.

Chapter 6

1. Benson, *Living Prayer,* 98.

2. Jane Rubietta, *Resting Place: A Personal Guide to Spiritual Retreats* (Downers Grove, Ill.: InterVarsity Press, 2005), 11-14.

3. Barton, *Invitation to Solitude and Silence,* 35.

4. Ibid., 37-42.

5. Henri J.M. Nouwen, *The Way of the Heart: Desert Spirituality and Contemporary Ministry* (San Francisco: HarperSanFrancisco, 1991), 81-82.

6. Kenneth Leech, *Experiencing God: Theology as Spirituality* (Eugene, Ore.: Wipf and Stock, 2002), 158.

7. Willard, *Hearing God,* 164.

8. Mark A. Moore, *The Rhythm of Prayer: A Forty Day Experience* (Indianapolis: Wesleyan Publishing House, 2006).

9. Nouwen, *Way of the Heart,* 69.

10. Ibid., 28.

11. Leech, *Experiencing God,* 156.

12. Ibid., 149.

13. Nouwen, *Way of the Heart,* 28.

14. Barton, *Invitation to Solitude and Silence,* 116.

15. Ibid., 132.

Chapter 7

1. Jerry Bridges, *Is God Really in Control? Trusting God in a World of Hurt,* (Colorado Springs: NavPress, 2006), 128.

2. Doug Greenwold, *Zechariah & Elizabeth* (Rockville, Md.: Bible-in-Context Ministries, 2004), 14.

3. Philip Yancey, *Disappointment with God: Three Questions No One Asks Aloud* (Grand Rapids: Zondervan, 1992), 270.

4. Ibid.

Chapter 8

1. Yancey, *Disappointment with God,* 123.

2. Willard, *Hearing God,* 112.

Chapter 9

1. Lawrence W. Wilson, *Why Me? Straight Talk About Suffering* (Kansas City: Beacon Hill Press of Kansas City, 2005), 44-46.

2. Willard, *Hearing God*, 205.
3. Ibid., 199.
4. Ibid., 200-201.
5. Yancey, *Disappointment with God*, 228.

Chapter 10

1. St. John of the Cross, *Dark Night of the Soul*, 35-36.
2. Ibid., 59.
3. Mirabai Starr, "Introduction" to St. John of the Cross, *Dark Night of the Soul* (New York, Riverhead Books, 2002), 10.
4. St. John of the Cross, *Dark Night of the Soul*, 69.
5. Yancey, *Disappointment With God*, 264.
6. Yancey, *Disappointment With God*, 188.
7. St. John of the Cross, *Dark Night of the Soul*, 56.
8. Barton, *Invitation to Solitude and Silence*, 117.

ACKNOWLEDGMENTS

I am grateful for all those at Beacon Hill Press who made this book possible. Bonnie Perry has been a particular source of encouragement, and I am also thankful for the help and support of Judi Perry and Barry Russell.

I also owe a large debt of gratitude to The Ninos, a group of Christian writers and artists to which I belong. They prayed for this book from the early idea stage to its completion. I would hate to tackle a book without them. Tom Allbaugh has been a steady friend and voice of sanity during our many discussions about writing and life. Diana Glyer has been an inspiration as I have witnessed her own dedication to writing and teaching. Other Ninos who have been particularly supportive in prayer during the writing of this book include Lynn Maudlin, Mike Glyer, Lois Carlson, Tim and Teresa Davis, Kayla Winiarz, and Liz Leahy. Paul Shrier has also been an encouraging supporter of my books.

I would like to thank Dick Pritchard and Laura Simmons for their friendship and for their help with some specific content in this book.

Steve Laube is my superb agent, and I am grateful for all the help he has given me.

I wish to thank my colleagues at Azusa Pacific University for all they have done to make this book and my other writing possible. Provost Michael Whyte has been a tremendous source of encouragement. My colleagues in the English Department have created an atmosphere of friendship and productivity that inspires me to keep writing. Special thanks go to

David Esselstrom, Glenys Gee, David Weeks, Diane Guido, and Carole Lambert.

The Spectrum class at Glendora Community Church allowed me to try out some of the ideas in this book on them as I was writing it. I appreciate their help and prayers, especially Steve and Debbie Singley, Steve and Lisa Jenne, Brent and Tina Cunningham, Rich and Marylee Nambu, Dick and Jackie Swinney, and Earl and Dianne Trout. I am also thankful for the thought-provoking and inspiring messages of our pastor, Mike Platter.

Without the support of my family, writing this or any other book would not be possible. I am grateful for the love of my parents and my sister Debbie. I also am particularly thankful for the love, support, and patience of my wife, Peggy, and my children, Jacob and Katie.

For more information, or to contact the author, please visit
www.josephbentz.com.